Diary of a Barrio Priest

Diary of a Barrio Priest

Michael P. Enright

ORBIS BOOKS
Maryknoll, New York 10545

Founded in 1970, Orbis Books endeavors to publish works that enlighten the mind, nourish the spirit, and challenge the conscience. The publishing arm of the Maryknoll Fathers and Brothers, Orbis seeks to explore the global dimensions of the Christian faith and mission, to invite dialogue with diverse cultures and religious traditions, and to serve the cause of reconciliation and peace. The books published reflect the views of their authors and do not represent the official position of the Maryknoll Society. To learn more about Maryknoll and Orbis Books, please visit our website at www.maryknoll.org.

Copyright © 2004 by Michael P. Enright

Published by Orbis Books, Maryknoll, NY 10545-0308.

Manufactured in the United States of America

Library of Congress Cataloging-in-Publication Data

Enright, Michael P.
  Diary of a barrio priest / Michael P. Enright.
     p.   cm.
  ISBN 1-57075-526-4 (pbk.)
  1. Enright, Michael P. 2. Catholic Church—Clergy—Biography. 3. Clergy—Illinois—Chicago—Biography. 4. Catholic Foreign Mission Society of America—Biography. I. Title.
  BX4705.E6635 A3 2004
  282'.092—dc22

                                    2003021602

*For all priests and religious
who shine the light of Christ
into the darkness*

I heard a Fly buzz—when I died—
The Stillness in the Room—
Was like the Stillness in the Air—
Between the Heavens of Storm—

The Eyes around—had wrung them dry—
And Breaths were gathering firm
For that last Onset—when the King
Be witnessed—in the Room—

I willed my Keepsakes—Signed away
What portion of me be
Assignable—and then it was
There interposed a Fly—

With Blue—uncertain stumbling Buzz—
Between the light—and me—
And then the Windows failed—and then
I could not see to see—

Emily Dickinson, c. 1882

Contents

Foreword

Father Enright has not written this book to engage in controversy with anyone. It is a personal story innocent of any ideological presuppositions, a story of a hard-working, happy priest who lives in a nightmare neighborhood, a free-fire zone, a place as dangerous as Beirut or Sarajevo were a few years ago, as Tel Aviv is today. It's also a story of how he has brought hope into the nightmare by reestablishing a parish structure that works, though its resources are pathetically meager. How much would have been accomplished, I wonder, in Immaculate Conception Parish if its pastor were not a man who knows what to do with a hammer and nails and a can of paint.

Though all stories are unique, there are many priests who live and work and bring hope in similar circumstances. Father Enright has the literary skill to tell a common enough story in a style that is both self-effacing and low-key and thus to bring hope not only to South Chicago but to all priests and all Catholics.

A friend of mine who read the manuscript for this book reported terrible dreams of shootouts and killings. I found myself murmuring prayers that Father Enright survives his remaining years at 88th and Commercial. I also wished often as I read the book that the Church would provide a little more help and support for him and other priests like him who are quite literally risking their lives for the work of the Gospel.

In the Chicago Archdiocese there are at least a million and a quarter Hispanics. The archdiocese cannot figure out what to do with them and for them. Father Enright is absolutely correct when he says that the biggest need these people have is a decent education for their children. His strategy of reopening the parish school with tuition virtually free is obvious enough. The old schools are still there in the barrio. The Catholic schools were the strongest resource the Church had to serve earlier immigrants. They can be a similar resource for the new immigrants. We don't have the money to do that, the Church replies.

Then one must say, in all candor, get the money.

Andrew Greeley

Preface

As good a place to start as any, I suppose, is being ordained a priest. I could tell you about the struggles I had going through the seminary... how I was convinced that the Lord had made a terrible mistake in calling me... how more than once I packed my bags to leave... how I doubted I could live as a celibate ... how much I enjoyed my seminary days... how I'd gotten through high school and college with the help of a few really dedicated padres, and how I'd been involved with women ... but that would make this into a three-volume book!

What I remember most of all is lying on the floor terrified. Part of the ceremony for ordination to the Catholic priesthood is that all the guys have to lie on the floor while the Church calls down the Holy Spirit to help us. I had a couple of good friends in the class, and they were crying for joy. I remember picking up my head and looking over and seeing the tears roll down their cheeks. I was more convinced than ever that I'd made a terrible mistake. When I had walked down the aisle that morning, my knees had almost been knocking. I thought seriously about turning around and running out of the seminary chapel, but my whole family was there, along with the seminary faculty and lots of friends.

Now I was lying on the sanctuary floor with my buddies around me, crying their eyes out for pure joy. And me here, absolutely terrified. If truth be told, I really didn't want to be a priest. It's just that I couldn't get the idea out of my head. No matter how hard I tried, it kept coming back to me that this was what the Lord wanted me to do. I suppose it's the feeling a fish gets when he's hooked.

If I could have had my own way, I'd much rather have been a truck driver with a big family and lots of kids. I've always had an easy time with mechanical things and I love to drive. I fought the Lord the whole time through the seminary ...and am still fighting with him occasionally! You might be surprised that a priest would fight with the Lord. It's just that lots of times he wants something done and I am unwilling to do it.

I was convinced on the day of my ordination that the Lord had made a mistake and have often thought the same thing since. He could have chosen someone holier, less pigheaded, and less passionate. But he chose me...and he's had to help me ever since.

My two best friends, the guys who were crying for joy, both left the priesthood within a couple of years of ordination. I'm still at it after eighteen years. I guess that's the pigheadedness coming through! Actually, I'm really happy doing what I'm doing and can't imagine living a life I don't love. But it wasn't easy getting to this point. This book is about my journey. It's about the people I've lived with and worked with, and it's about God's grace.

First Confessions
Or, The First Day on the Job for the New Priest

In May of 1984 I was ordained. I'd been assigned to St. Mark's parish with Ed Maloney, an old-timer who was considered a good priest. He was.

Being new, I had a set of expectations about parish life, about my living space, about who and what I was and about what I could and should do. I'd spent the past few years learning Spanish during the summers between classes at the seminary. I'd lived with a Mexican family for a summer and spent a couple of summers at language schools, and I'd come to love Hispanic culture. I was ready.

Actually, looking back on the whole situation, I was pretty arrogant. I thought being a priest was about what I could do. I was ready to change the world, make it a better place, help people, preach the Gospel, and give my life away in service to the Kingdom. I've learned some things since then. Not all of them were easy to learn. As my father used to say, quoting somebody famous, "Knowledge makes a bloody entrance."

In retrospect I'm truly amazed at the assumptions I was making. Imagine a lawyer joining a law firm, fresh from passing the bar exam, and thinking he's the peer of the senior partner at the firm. Or a doctor fresh out of medical school thinking he's as good as a physician who's been practicing medicine for thirty years. That was my problem, as I look back. I thought I was Ed's equal. And I wasn't.

Immediately on arrival at St. Mark's, I had a look at my rooms in the rectory. They were pretty rough looking. Being

1

new, I insisted that they had to be painted, that new carpet had to be put in and some new furniture gotten. After all, I deserved all this, didn't I? I was the new priest!

The rectory was ancient, maybe a hundred years old, and had seen better days. In its glory days it must have been quite a place—ten-foot ceilings, hardwood trim all over the place, arched doorways, and all the other features that make old houses in Chicago worth rehabbing. Over the years, the wood had been painted brown, dark paneling had been put over all the walls to cover cracks in the plaster, what had been elegant mini-parlors by the first floor entrance had been turned into offices, and half-hearted attempts had been made to upgrade the bathrooms. In other words, the place had survived about fifteen pastors since being built. It had once been in the heart of a middle-class neighborhood. That had changed.

St. Mark's was now a ghetto parish, and there is never enough money in ghetto parishes. Sometimes the pastor wonders whether he'll have enough money to make payroll from week to week. Still, Ed had been to the "pastors of newly ordained" workshop and told he should be "kind" to me, so he agreed to have my rooms painted and get new carpet. He also told me I could buy some new furniture when I got back from Mexico. Then off I went to spend the summer studying Spanish.

I'd been working on learning Spanish for the past few summers, and this was to be the last blast, a kind of final touch to my speaking and understanding the language. I never even considered that Ed might wonder about paying a salary for someone who was off taking Spanish lessons and not working in the parish.

When I arrived back at the parish, I was pretty wiped out. I'd taken the Tecolote from Mexico City. It's the "owl" flight, the one that leaves daily at around midnight from Mexico to O'Hare. I arrived at around 4:00 in the morning and found my room locked. I couldn't find a place to sleep, so I crashed on the floor of a spare room until around 7:00, when Ed woke up and I got a key to my room.

I'd expected to find the room painted and the junk pretty well cleared out of there. Instead, I found a mess. I started unpacking and then tried to find somewhere to put my stuff. Most of that day, which was a Saturday, I spent trying to get organized. At 5:00, Ed told me to "go hear confessions." It was time to go to work.

I didn't have keys to the church, or to anything else other than my room yet. I hadn't slept the night before and hadn't really had anything to eat all day. I was pretty crabby, thinking about how Ed was a nasty and heartless priest. "I don't have keys," I said to him. "How do I get in there?"

"Rose will let you in."

So, off I went, half grumbling about how this was no way to treat a new priest. I hadn't yet been inside the church and had no real idea what it even looked like. You have to imagine the new padre leaving the rectory with one of those little black cartoon clouds over his head as he grumbles to himself.

When I got to the church I found the side door locked. I was feeling terrified of the whole deal and was a little disappointed already. So I stood there, banging on the door. Finally, a woman came and opened it. I told her I was the new priest and she let me in.

I went over to the confessional and had a look. This confessional was the "traditional" kind, with three doors next to each other in a row. The middle door was for the padre and the two side doors were for the penitents (the people going to confession). I'd never been inside the "middle box" of a confessional and had to check it out. We hadn't dealt with this in the confession practicum, I thought. More grumbling.

When I got inside, I saw that there were little grilles through which the penitent and the priest could speak to each other, and little sliding doors to ensure the privacy of the conversations. I sat down in the priest's chair and worked the sliding doors on either side. Simple enough, I thought. Then I had a look at the electrical switches. From what I remember, there were five switches located just inside the door of the little box I was sitting in. I tried the first one and nothing happened. I left the box to check the lights outside. On a confessional, there are pilot lights above each door, red and green. They're to tell the penitents whether there's a priest in there, and above the side doors they tell the people whether the box on that side is "occupied."

I went back inside the box and tried another switch. Again, nothing. By now, I was beginning to panic. I couldn't even work the little lights. I didn't want to call Rose over and ask her about the lights. Who wants to be completely incompetent in front of a stranger?

Finally, I figured out the damn switches. One was for a fan that would suck out the air in the confessional. The motor was somewhere up in the attic of the church, connected by ducts to the box. That way, the noise it made wouldn't be heard. The other switches were for the lights—a master power switch and three that changed the color of the pilot lights from red to green. I played with them for a while and finally got the one over my door to "green" and the ones over the side doors to "green" too. I didn't need the fan, since it was dark, quiet, and cool in the box.

Now, I'm sitting there. I pray a little bit so I'll be a good confessor. Every once in a while I try the switches to be sure I have the working of them down cold. Then the door to one of the side boxes opens. I can feel the pressure change and a little "whoosh" of air as the door closes and the person kneels down. I change the switch for that side to "red" and slide the little door open, ready to listen, perhaps give a little advice, and then give a penance and forgive the person's sin in the name of Jesus. I'm sweating by now, and the person hasn't even started.

There's a whisper. Something I can't make out. "Uh huh," I answer. Then the person starts talking more. I say to the person (I can't make out if it's a man or a woman), "Could you please speak a little louder?" She does. It turns out she's elderly. She's talking away, and I can't make heads or tails out of what she's saying to me. I don't understand a single word. I'm wondering what's wrong with me. "Blah blah ba blah blah." Pause. I answer her, "Uh-huh." She continues, "Blah blah BLAH ba blah." By now I'm really sweating.

I ask her if she's sorry for her sins, and she answers, "Yes." I give her a penance and absolution. She gets up to leave and I slide the little door on her side closed. I'm thinking, "That was a disaster. What was the use of all that language study?"

While she's been confessing, someone has come into the other side. I pause to take a breath. Then I lean over and slide the little door open. The person starts talking. At least this one talks louder. In fact, he's so loud I'm wondering if everyone in the church can hear him. He's elderly and, I take it, hard of hearing. The only problem is, I can't understand him either. "Bla ba blah. BLAH ba blah blah." By now I'm praying to Jesus. What is this? I ask the man if he's sorry for his sins and he says, "Yes." Penance and absolution. He gets up to leave. My first two confessions in my new parish, and I don't know if I've given someone "two Hail Marys" as a penance for an axe murder, or what.

By now I'm really sweating in the little box. I'm completely soaked, right down to my socks. I have the feeling I can't breathe. Time to find the switch for that fan. I turn on the fan and realize I haven't moved the switches for the little lights. Which way is red, which is green? I open the door of the box and stand outside. I lean back into the box and switch the damn things back and forth. The lights are toggling "red-green-red-green." I set all the lights to green.

I'm standing in the doorway of the confessional when a little old lady walks up to me. She says something like "Hello. You must be the new priest." I can hardly make out what she's saying. "Yes, I'm Father Mike." She's Puerto Rican. Most of the parish is Puerto Rican...I knew that. She doesn't have any teeth, either. I gather that she was the first penitent.

Mexican Spanish is very different from Puerto Rican Spanish. I later learn that in every country where Spanish is spoken there's a different accent, that sometimes Mexicans have a difficult time understanding Puerto Ricans and vice versa, that there are regional differences in pronunciation within some Latin countries, and that idiomatic expressions are unusually difficult. I'll need a whole set of other "language facts" that will enable me to talk to and understand any Spanish speaker.

For now, I'm instantly learning that my "Mexican" Spanish is going to be pretty much useless around here. This Puerto Rican Spanish is almost unintelligible to me. It sounds like the ends of all the words are dropped and the rhythm of the language is nothing at all like Mexican Spanish. I've just gotten off the plane from Mexico, where I've had six weeks of language study. It was something like my fourth dose of the language. I've been feeling confident that I'll be able to pretty well understand anyone. And now here's this little old Puerto Rican lady, a saint, I'm sure. She's talking away at me with no teeth. I'm standing in the doorway of the confessional and I can make out maybe one word in ten. It sounds like she's talking with a mouth full of marbles.

She smiles and says, "Welcome to the parish." At least, that's what I think she says. She senses that I'm uneasy and she reaches out and puts her hand on mine. She pats my hand a little and tells me it will be okay.

I go back into the box. I'm sitting there thinking about how I'm incapable of doing this. I'm begging Jesus to help me do a good job. He doesn't seem to be answering me. Finally, the last of the people for confession comes through and I'm done for the day.

My first day on the job, and I've failed miserably. That's what I thought as I left the church. When I got back to the rectory, Ed must have asked me how it went, and I must have answered, "Fine." That turned out to be my pattern early on in priesthood. I'd fail at one or another thing, someone would ask me how it went, and I'd answer, "Fine."

I wasn't quite ready to accept my radical incompetence to do this job. Early on, I thought it was all about me, and what I could do. Looking back, I wish I'd known different. I guess it would take some more slaps from reality before I'd learn. That day, I thanked God I had gotten back to the rectory without having done any more damage to anyone.

The First Time I Almost Got Killed

The first time I almost got killed, I was a block away from St. Mark's. I'd been in the parish as a new padre for a couple of weeks. Since my rooms needed to be cleaned out and painted, I'd been helping with the work. Still, I had a bad attitude about it. It wasn't that I couldn't paint and plaster. It was simply that I thought someone else should be doing the work. I was a PADRE, after all!

It was a sunny afternoon and I decided I'd go for a walk. I'd heard a few gunshots at night already, but it was daytime and I wanted to go and see how the neighborhood was doing. It was what you were supposed to do, get to know the "lay of the land," so to speak.

I walked down the street on the north end of the parish, heading west. I stopped to visit one of the families I knew lived on the block. It was a hot afternoon. Up and down the block, people were on their porch steps, catching a little of the breeze. There were little kids riding their tricycles on the sidewalk and playing in the grass between the sidewalk and the street. There were mothers and grandmothers dressed in the coolest housecoats they could find, sitting on their concrete steps and fanning themselves. There were groups of young girls standing in the shady spots, trying to look cool for the young guys who were cruising by on bikes or walking on the sidewalk.

The family I'd gone to visit—I don't remember their name —wasn't home, so I stood talking with some kids I'd seen the Sunday before at Mass. It was a good chance to practice Puerto

Rican Spanish. It was wonderful and peaceful, standing there talking to the neighbors.

Then this kid comes running down the block from the church building toward me. He seems to have something in his had. I just stand there, looking at him. He gets up to me and stops right behind me. I'm too startled to move, but I look down at his hand and think I see a gun. A chrome gun.

He fires one shot, right next to me. It's very loud. He's shooting at someone who's running into an alley between two houses, and I'm his shield. I dive for the sidewalk, and he shoots two or three more times right over the top of me.

I'm lying on the sidewalk with my ears ringing, praying to Jesus. "Not now, Lord. I have a summer program to run. Not now."

It's all over in a second. I look up and right in front of me is a tricycle, overturned, with the front wheel still spinning. I slowly start to get up, and there's nobody anywhere to be seen. I'm immediately reminded of one of those Westerns where the gunslinger comes into town and all you can see is closed windows and tumbleweeds blowing down the street. I stand up. I'm a little shaky. The people slowly start to come out of their houses and go back to sitting on the stoop. They had the sense, I realize now, to recognize danger and get out of the way. You might think that's automatic, but I've found that the opposite can be true. Sometimes your first instinct is dead wrong. I froze. The people on the block ran away. They were smarter, but I would learn. If I lived long enough!

I had a meeting scheduled that night. I called everyone and cancelled the meeting. I've found since then that nearly getting killed can ruin the rest of the day. It's another of those things they didn't tell me in the seminary.

A couple of days later, I was on the way home from the hospital where I'd gone to visit somebody who was sick. In those days, not every car had air-conditioning. Mine didn't, and the sun was beating down on me. I can remember sweating like a pig. I glanced down at the black clergy shirt plastered to my arm as it hung out the window of the driver's door and it occurred to me that this was the perfect color to get you broiled in your car. I was also thinking how about great it was to be alive, and enjoying the sensation of roasting away.

I arrived back at the rectory and went up to my room. It was gradually beginning to look habitable, thank God. I sat down, turned on the TV, and began to think about life here at St. Mark's. I did a lot of thinking in those days, getting used to being a priest. Thank God I had a retreat scheduled for soon after this first incident of almost being killed. If I hadn't gone on that retreat, I wouldn't have been able to function at all in the kind of environment that can become suddenly deadly—the kind I've been in for the past eighteen years!

As the days turned into weeks, then months at St. Mark's, it became clear that things weren't going well between Ed and me. I wasn't ready to accept that I needed to learn how to be a priest, that I needed to learn even the most basic things. I remember one staff meeting with the deacons, early on in my assignment at St. Mark's. We were going to begin the meeting by praying a decade of the rosary. Each person had to pray a Hail Mary, one of the most basic prayers Catholics know. I panicked. I'd never learned the Hail Mary in Spanish, and so I was listening with 110 percent attention as the others prayed. When it was my turn, I turned red and started to sweat. I hadn't been able to learn it by listening a few times to other people praying it. I thought Ed had purposely picked this way to humiliate me. Of course, I had that towering arrogance thing going!

At the time, Placido Rodriguez lived upstairs in the back of the rectory. He was a bishop, and a decent guy. I started complaining to him about Ed, and he'd always listen patiently. At one point, he told me what he'd told his first pastor. It was something like, "You're a good pastor, and I hope to be one someday. I hope to learn all I can from you."

By then, things between Ed and me had deteriorated to the point that we were barely speaking. I thought Placido's comment was absolute nonsense. Of course, in retrospect, I realize that he was right. I had a whole lot to learn, but I didn't think so then.

One of the things I had to learn was how to deal with gangs and death. I'm still working on that one, but the first incident is always pretty memorable. If I'd have been on better terms with Ed, I could have asked him what to do. As it was, I had to learn on the fly.

My First Jumper

It was a funeral for a Spanish Cobra—a gang member. I hadn't dealt with this kind of thing before and I wasn't exactly sure of what to do at the wake.

The funeral home had seen better days. The front doors were badly in need of a coat of paint. The plastic flowers near the entrance hadn't been cleaned in years. The carpet was worn through to the backing. Gathered in the hallway was a crowd of gangbangers wearing black and green. A cop stood by the door.

I later learned that wakes are an ideal time for gang activities, like revenge, etc. It's part of the whole deal. Smart funeral directors don't take gang funerals at all. The ones who do accept these funerals usually hire an off-duty cop to stand in a prominent place and try to keep a lid on things.

As I started the service, I was glad to be a Catholic. We don't have to make up prayers everytime someone dies. We can just use the "Ritual for a Wake" and go on autopilot. The ritual itself carries everybody along. Thank God, because the mother of the kid and his girlfriend were really crying as I said the final prayers.

I managed to get through the wake and the funeral Mass. I'm not exactly sure how I did it. It's almost impossible to talk when you're choked up. It must have been God's grace at work.

At the cemetery, that's where things broke down a little bit. The Cobras were all gathered around, and it sure seemed to be a gathering of evil. The guy's mom was there, and, quietly weeping, his grandmother too.

We're all standing around the casket as it is slowly lowered into the ground. Then the girlfriend starts wailing.

She's going to jump into the hole with her boyfriend. People are trying to stop her, and there's general mayhem all around me. The only person who's calm is the funeral director. I motion to him, a gesture meant to say something like, "Aren't you going to do something?" He comes over and pulls me a short distance away from the open grave.

"Father, I've seen this more times than you can count." He looks over to the crowd. "They should just let her jump. She won't do it. It's all a show. What a surprise it would be for her if they just let her go!" He laughs a little. He can see that I'm a little shocked still.

"Father," he goes on in a low voice, "this guy was probably a bastard while he was alive and she probably hated him. It's all fake."

I go back to the parish with him, and on the way he tells me tales of things that have happened at funerals. Ever since then, if somebody wants to jump into the hole with the dead guy, I just step back.

Leaving St. Mark's

After about a year and a half at St. Mark's parish, it became clear to me that things weren't working out with Ed and that the situation probably wasn't going to get any better. I've since learned that for quite a few of us guys, our first assignment is very difficult and many of us leave the parish before our assigned term has come to an end. I think it has to do with expectations of what priesthood and parish life will be like, and the clash of those expectations with reality.

In this case it wasn't too difficult to get a change. I called the priest in charge of the assignment process and told him I had to leave St. Mark's. Since this was not during the "usual" transition time, I was told to go and talk to John Manz, the pastor of Blessed Agnes Parish on 26th Street.

The person I was when I went to see John was very different from the person I had been when I first went to St. Mark's. I was pretty well shaken by the failure I'd experienced with Ed (he was a good priest and somehow he and I couldn't make things work) and I had a very different set of expectations about parish life and rectory living and priesthood than I'd had at the outset. As I made my way down to 26th Street, I figured that if I couldn't make it this assignment work, I'd probably leave and get married and become a truck driver. I'd have to find a wife, though.

I met John for lunch at one of the Mexican restaurants in his neighborhood. I'll never forget the conversation, or the first impression I had of him. He was a big guy with a gruff voice, not a person to mince words, and not a particularly "nice" guy. Over our *caldo de camarones* (shrimp soup) he asked me, "So, what's wrong with you? How come you couldn't get along with Ed Maloney?" I just about spit into my soup. What could I say? I did my best to tell him what had happened, and at the end of the conversation he said something like, "Okay. Why don't you think about this a little? I'll also think about it a little and we'll talk in a day or two." Here I was, ready to move in, and he was telling me to "think about it a little." I guess he had to do what a smart pastor usually does—call someone and ask for the lowdown on this stranger.

A couple of days later we spoke again, and I ended up going to Blessed Agnes. I moved in, as I've said, with very different expectations about parish life, rectory life, and being a priest. This time, I was glad to be given a couple of gallons of paint and a brush, and glad to go to work painting my room. This rectory was newer than the one at St. Mark's. It had been built in the late 1950s and was tiny in comparison with St. Mark's. It had eight-foot ceilings, cement floors with tile on them, and smaller rooms. Still, the walls were brick and solid enough. After I'd painted the sitting room, bedroom, and bathroom, some of the kids helped me carry my stuff upstairs. I put my books on the shelves built into the wall and went to work.

It seemed that things were going well. Then I had the first of a few "conversations" with John.

One Sunday afternoon, we were in the rectory and he called me into the front office. I sensed that something was up. He asked me what I'd preached about. I told him I had spoken about a friend of mine who'd lost her child.

"What was your friend's name?" he asked.

"Maria."

"Oh," he said. "Then you didn't say that the Virgin Mary had an abortion and that Jesus had lots of brothers and sisters."

I turned red. I was speechless. "No," I managed to say.

"Well, that's what someone heard. Not only one person. A group of women are in the other office, and that's what they heard."

I couldn't figure it out. Not at all. What had I said? Then it occurred to me. The word for "miscarriage" in Spanish is *aborto*. Unfortunately, that is the same as the word for "abortion." These women had heard me say that the Virgin Mary had an abortion (what a poor choice, naming my friend "Mary" in the example I used in the homily!) and that Jesus had brothers and sisters. I tried to explain to John, and he went and made peace with the ladies. It was the first of many times when John ran interference for me as I made all the mistakes you might expect from someone new on the job.

Some of the language mistakes I made were pretty outrageous. I think it's what happens when you're trying to learn a language and you pick up little expressions you think are idiomatic. When I was working at St. Mark's, a Spaniard would come and stay for the summer. One of his favorite expressions was *coño*. He used it as if it meant "golly," or "gosh," and so I picked it up. It didn't bother the Puerto Ricans too much. I think they thought it strange that I'd use the word, but it was no big deal. Blessed Agnes, however, was a Mexican parish, and Mexicans think *coño* . . . well, it's about the foulest word you can think of to describe female parts. Thank God I didn't use that word at Mass. There were some other ones, though.

One Sunday I was preaching about how we imagine the devil. "You know," I said in Spanish, "a little red man with pointy ears and long fingernails and a tail." As I said this, I pointed to where a tail ought to go. The expression on the people's faces and the little giggles from the kids told me I'd said something wrong. I went on as if nothing had happened and afterward asked someone what had been so funny. It turns out that *cola* is "tail" and *culo* is something else entirely. I had switched the words and said *culo*, which is the crude way of saying "anus." No wonder they were giggling. It's not a "church" word.

I made the same mistake again (no, I don't learn from my mistakes) at a meeting of parents getting ready for baptism. Unfortunately, the word *cola* can also mean "line." Here was a big group of people and I wanted to tell them to form a line, beginning at the registration table. So, of course, I pointed to the table and told them to form themselves "into an asshole," beginning right there. They were stunned. At least they didn't laugh out loud.

These stories aren't the worst, though. The worst was one incident that I'll remember for as long as I live. It had all the ingredients for a completely humiliating and embarrassing moment, and I charged right into it.

It was a meeting of a few young couples and one of the nuns working in the parish. We met in the front office of the rectory, a smallish room jammed with ten people. I don't even remember what the meeting was about.

At one point, one of the guys said he was having trouble with his back. A priest friend of mine had been having a similar problem and he'd gone for a *sobada*. That's a massage, and there's usually someone in every Mexican neighborhood who knows how to work the kinks out of your muscles and bones. Unfortunately, *soplada* is not the same word. *Soplada* is a crude expression for oral sex, as I soon found out. So, at this meeting with a few young couples and a nun, out it comes.

"Why don't you tell your wife to give you a *soplada*?" I could hear a collective sharp intake of breath and, not being one to stop when the stopping was good, I went on, "That's what they're for, isn't it? When you come home with a sore back, you just ask your wife to give you a *soplada* and you feel better, right?"

I thought I was talking about a massage. By now, an absolute silence had settled on the room. The nun was red, red, red. The couples were all looking at the floor, and I realized I must have said something hideously wrong.

"What did I say?" I asked.

Nobody answered. Nobody would even look at me. They stared at the floor in shocked embarrassment. It suddenly got really hot in the office.

"What?"

I had to wait until the meeting was over, and then one of the men finally explained. The shock of shame knocked the wind out of me.

It's taken me some time, but I've more or less mastered the language by now. The learning of it was something else, that's for sure. I've made thousands of mistakes, and continue to do so, almost every Sunday. Still, the people have been very patient. I guess this learning and working in another language thing has given me great empathy for someone who tries to learn English. At least Spanish is pretty regular. English, if you take the time to think about it, is nearly impossible. Consider a word like "lead." It's a metal, it's the present tense of a verb ("I lead the group every Sunday"), and it's a noun that's not the metal ("Do you have a lead on the job?"). I've often thought that it's a good thing I learned English as a kid.

In any case, I managed after a couple of years to learn Spanish well enough to function. There were lots of other things I had to learn before I was ready to be a pastor, and one of them was how to deal with evil.

Evil

You might think a priest would have to know about evil, having gone through four years of theology studies and a total of twelve years of seminary education. I guess they just figured we already knew about it. I don't remember evil ever being mentioned in any class, and I'm American enough to have thought evil was a fiction...somehow not quite real. I don't know exactly what I thought I was dealing with as I buried young man after young man killed in the gang warfare that was continual at St. Mark's and at Blessed Agnes, but I certainly hadn't named it evil.

By the time I had the experience I'm about to tell you about, I'd been at Blessed Agnes for around four years. I'd been pretty active working with the young people and I had also spent some time walking the streets and talking to the gang members I'd see on the corners. They were without exception respectful and they seemed to listen. Knowing I was from the church, they seemed to realize I'd have to bury them one day and deal with their families. I had also taken to painting a white cross on the sidewalk near where someone had been killed. I wanted the community to recognize the spot, so I'd find out where the person had died (it didn't matter what gang they were from) and go and paint a white cross on the sidewalk. I'd heard that some of the gang leaders weren't happy with me, and wanted to kill me...but those were only rumors.

So, one night we were having "scripture and basketball" in the parish gym. The pastor, John, was on vacation, and I think in the two weeks he was gone I might have buried two or three kids. In any case, this was a Thursday night and there must have been close to a hundred kids in the hall. We'd look at the Gospel for the coming Sunday, break into groups and discuss it, and then have a large group meeting so they could ask questions. After that they could play basketball. Dee LaCour, a Cajun woman, and a few other adults were helping run this program, and they were proud of it. How else could you get a hundred kids at a time to have some contact with the Lord?

After the kids had finished talking about the scriptures and were starting to play ball, I noticed a group standing on the sidelines. I went over to talk to them. I recognized them . . . they were all kids who came every Thursday night. When I asked them their names, their answers were something like, "Shorty, Lefty, Beto, Pee Wee, and Lucky." These were beautiful young people. They looked like angels, and here they were learning about the Bible and playing ball. I felt great. As I said, I'd buried a couple of kids during John's absence and I'd had more than my share of violence and the bad feelings that go with gang funerals. Here was a group of kids looking to learn something about the Gospel and have some fun. It was something hopeful in the midst of all the crap that was going on.

Suddenly, I thought of asking them if they were in gangs. I don't know why I even asked the question. Maybe I wanted to reassure myself that what I was doing was making a difference.

Shorty answered first. "I'm a King."

Then Lefty said, "Me, too."

Beto told me he was a "Two-Six" and they went around the circle telling me their various allegiances. After Shorty's response, I had a cold feeling in my stomach. By the time the last kid had spoken, I had what Mexicans call "chicken skin." The hairs on my arms and the back of my neck were standing up. My gut felt frozen, and I could almost hear cold, cruel laughter.

I guess it's hard to understand this kind of feeling if you've never experienced it. It was as if the floor had opened up into a huge hole and all the life and light were being sucked down into it. Here were these kids, looking like angels on a Christmas card, and they were telling me they were all gangbangers. It made a mockery of all my efforts and the efforts of everyone else working with this group. It felt like being hit with a sledge-hammer. I ran out of air and told them I'd see them later...and then I went outside so I could breathe.

For the next couple of days, I was really in a foul mood. My sense of humor was completely gone. I couldn't stop thinking about what had happened. I kept imagining having the funerals for these kids, and I found myself shuffling around as if I had the weight of the world on my shoulders.

The following Sunday night, John came home from his vacation. I'd wanted to talk to him from the very night this happened. I figured he'd been around a long time and he could tell me what was wrong with me.

We always got together in the living room to watch the news at 10:00, so that night I told him about how I was feeling and asked him what he thought.

"Oh," he said, hardly looking away from the TV screen, "That's just evil."

"Evil? You mean like the devil?"

"Of course," he answered, as he took a sip of his beer. This was old hat for him, and he wasn't making too much of the whole thing.

I sat there and thought about the icy weight that had been gripping my insides, about how I had been unable to laugh at all for about three days, about how I had been obsessing about what had happened, and about how I had been feeling "gotten a hold of," if you know what I mean. Then I started getting afraid. I looked over at him and said something like, "So, you mean to tell me the devil exists?"

He put his glass down and gave me his undivided attention, "Of course." He paused. "What did they teach you guys at the seminary, anyway?"

"I guess I knew there was a devil...but I've never felt this before."

The next day I went off to find Fr. Jim Doyle. He was a scripture professor at the seminary and I remembered that he was a very holy guy. I also remembered that he was now working as a hospital chaplain at St. Anthony's and I desperately wanted to get make some sense of this evil thing. If I'd thought about evil before this, it had been as a kind of generic darkness. I had never experienced a personal "attack" and I wasn't sure I could survive this. I felt really bad—sad and frustrated and angry and obsessing all at once. I couldn't seem to shake myself free from it and I figured he'd give me good advice. He did!

As I sat in his office he almost laughed at me. How naive, he said, to think that I could be a priest and not run across evil. He told me that clearly the devil exists, and that there are malignant spirits out there, too. Then he told me not to worry, that the power of Christ and the grace of my own baptism, the Eucharist, my confirmation, and holy orders would protect me. I still wasn't convinced and told him so.

He said, "The devil was castrated when Jesus rose from the dead." I burst out laughing. Doyle was always pretty earthy...maybe that's why I liked him so much. He said that evil could startle us, like the flash from a camera, but that there was no real power there, and that I should count on God's grace and power.

I left there feeling a whole lot better. Still, I wanted to know more about all this, so I made an appointment to see Fr. John Canary. He had been my spiritual director in the seminary and we still kept in touch. When I met with him this time, he explained a little more about evil and then he gave me some advice.

"Whenever you find evil, don't engage it. Run away."

I told him I wasn't too happy with that advice. He explained that it was easy to get sucked into a fight I'd be bound to lose, and that I should stay away from evil. How can you fight a shadow?

I got back to the parish and started doing some reading. I found a book called *People of the Lie,* by Scott Peck. In it, he details how some people simply do evil, and there's really very little anyone can do about it. I looked at a couple of other books and prayed about the question of evil for several weeks. I started feeling better...less "gotten a hold of" and more able to laugh at jokes. I thought I had this thing down...that I knew how to deal with evil. Not quite. Even now, after eighteen years a priest, I find myself surprised by the various forms that attacks of evil can take.

I have some thoughts on evil. You shouldn't take this as definite truth, I think, and not all priests will agree with this. In fact, in the middle of all this early learning, I joined a priest's prayer and support group and brought up the subject. One of the padres in the group told me he thought I needed to go see a psychologist. So, not all padres will agree with this...

Evil exists. The devil exists. But he's not like you imagine him. He's much more subtle and intelligent than a little red man with a tail! All you have to do is think about it for a minute. If the devil showed up looking hideous and frightening, the first thing anyone would do is run away. No, he's much too smart to show his true colors. So, how do you know when you're running into evil?

I think there are some clues you can find in your heart, or maybe in the patterns of your life. The biggest clues have to do with laughter, freedom, and wholeness. I think it's worth looking at these clues, because sometimes we find ourselves with a feeling that "something's wrong" and we can't quite put our finger on the problem.

Perhaps the clearest clue that there's some evil floating around is when we lose our sense of humor. I think our spirits react to evil by going on the defensive, and suddenly we find ourselves unable to laugh at ourselves or jokes or anything. I guess the nature of evil is that it wants to convince us that the situation we're involved in is absolute, in other words, that there's really nothing else out there that's important or valuable. One of the functions of humor, I think, is to remind us that there's another reality out there. Evil doesn't like that, because if we don't give the situation our absolute attention we may be able to step back into freedom.

Freedom, or the lack of freedom, is the second clue that there's some evil around. You may have heard of "possession." That's when evil gets a total hold on someone. I've learned that there's a step before possession, and it's called obsession. If you find yourself obsessed, you can be sure there's some evil involved. If you can't stop thinking about a situation, if you find yourself getting filled with rage or despair, if you find yourself feeling that "something's got a hold of me," you're possibly looking at some evil. The devil hates laughter, because then you're not taking him seriously enough, and freedom, because he wants complete ownership of situations and people. If you have your freedom, you can move toward wholeness.

Perhaps the most important clue about the presence of evil has to do with integrity, or wholeness. The scriptural word for evil is *diablos,* a Greek word that has to do with bowling. Bowling? Yes, bowling. *Bole* is "to throw," and *diablos* is "to throw apart." The opposite is *symbolos,* which means "to throw together." If you find yourself being torn apart, you may be looking at some evil.

I think you have to take all these things together. Imagine a situation in which you lose your sense of humor and are convinced that it's deadly serious. Then you slowly lose your freedom and begin to feel that you're in a trap. Then you feel sad and angry and torn in half. Have you ever felt that way? Maybe it was evil.

What is the goal of all this activity on the part of evil? I think it's to distract us from doing what we can. At least that's what I've found many times in my encounters with evil. Somehow, something gets a hold of you, and you find yourself paralyzed and sad, feeling alone. And you can't seem to find what to do. You've lost your perspective, nothing strikes you as funny, and you don't have the energy to do anything at all. From the point of view of the spirit, the devil has you where he wants you.

I'd learned some things about evil in my work at Blessed Agnes. It was a good thing, because soon enough I'd be the pastor of a parish. Then the real fun would start!

South Chicago

If you look at a map of Chicago, you may not even see South
Chicago. A lot of maps of the city stop at 67th Street, at the
southern end of the parks that run along the lakeshore. I'd
never been in the neighborhood until I started working here
back in 1993. It's pretty well cut off from the rest of the city,
and a place you wouldn't probably "go visit" unless you had a
good reason. I arrived at Immaculate Conception after being
asked repeatedly by the local bishop to come and work here. I
suppose a few words of explanation are needed about that.

You might think priests are assigned to parishes. That's not
the case here in Chicago. At least not for the most part. When
a parish is without a pastor, there's a process the archdiocese
goes through to try and find a pastor. The parish is "open
listed." That means that every priest in the archdiocese re-
ceives a description of the parish and is invited to consider becoming the pastor. The parishes that are perceived as "plums"
get a lot of applicants. Those are the places that have some
money, usually suburban parishes without a lot of problems.
They generally have only one ethnic group—usually white
people—and only one language. The less desirable parishes
are the ones in the city, and even less desirable are city
parishes with multiple ethnic groups and no money. The way
the system works, an inner-city parish can go for months without anyone considering applying for the pastorate.

Then the local bishop begins to "network" to try and find
someone to take the parish. The archdiocese of Chicago is divided into six "vicariates" and each of them has a bishop in

charge. In the case of Immaculate Conception, Wilton Gregory was the bishop in charge at the time. I knew him from the seminary, where he taught liturgy classes. He called me a few times and I finally agreed to come and serve as the temporary administrator.

The plan was for me to eventually be replaced by a religious order priest. A religious community—I don't remember if it was the Franciscans or the Dominicans or who—was considering taking the parish over in a kind of a "trade." The archdiocese had given them permission to build a new parish out in the suburbs on the condition that they staff an inner-city parish. Immaculate Conception was the inner-city parish they had to staff in exchange for permission to build in suburbia.

The parish had a whole lot of internal problems, and the environment in the neighborhood was pretty tough. All the previous pastors had each left before the end of their terms. One had left after ten years, with two years to go on his second term as pastor. The next got a brain tumor after six months, and the next was attacked by chronic diarrhea after three months.

In I waltzed. I thought I'd seen a tough neighborhood at Blessed Agnes where I had served for six and a half years, and St. Mark's, where I'd been for a year and a half. I'd been a priest for eleven years and thought I was ready.

I was in for a surprise.

It turned out that within the block-and-a-half radius of the church there were six gangs fighting over territory. They're still here today. They had drawn their line at 88th Street and Commercial Avenue. Unfortunately, that's the corner the church sits on. Not only that, but the neighborhood had been pretty well devastated by the closing of the steel mills in the 1970s. What used to be a prosperous neighborhood where you were guaranteed a job at $20 an hour as soon as you graduated from high school was turning into something very different.

The internal parish dynamics had been pretty well shaken up, too. There were the "old timers," primarily of Polish descent. Then there were the Mexicans. And they weren't getting along. The Mexican community was divided, and the old-time Polish community was standing off on the sidelines, watching to see what would happen. There had been five parishes in the neighborhood and, as a result of changing demographics and economic stresses, these shrank to two. Anyone who had the money to leave when the mills closed did so. The archdiocese had optimistically approved the creation of a "parish coopera-tive," a kind of hybrid parish where there were supposed to be five sites and a centralized administration.

The archdiocese had promised at the time of the creation of the cooperative that "no parish would be closed." The prom-ise was not kept. The remnant of the parish cooperative was Immaculate Conception. It was a hurting parish, with a lot of anger and resentment stored up, and a real mistrust of the archdiocese. My predecessor, the one who got chronic diar-rhea, had tried to make a go of it. In the end, the people from the archdiocesan Office of Conciliation had walked out of the parish after two meetings designed to help people "express their feelings." These South Chicago people expressed their feelings, all right. It wasn't pretty. The conciliators gave up and washed their hands of the situation. Then the padre left, and the parish sat there abandoned.

I was in for a surprise. After I had been in the parish for a few weeks, a group of Mexican parishioners got together and wrote to Wilton Gregory, the local bishop. They said they were concerned about a few things, and asked the bishop to remove me as the pastor. I hadn't even been named pastor yet. I was just the temporary administrator. And they wanted me gone.

Wilton had already been through a whole lot with my predecessor and so he completely backed me up. He didn't want to lose another pastor and go through the hassle of trying to find some other guy to take the place. If he hadn't stood up for me, I would have happily walked away and who knows what would have happened to Immaculate Conception. As it was, there were rumors that the place might be closed. Wilton wrote back to the group and told them that they would have to make peace with me.

My nature being what it is, I came to the conclusion that I wanted to be the pastor of this parish. I saw that these people were desperate for a pastor. I couldn't see them going another day without a pastor, let alone six or eight months. I also didn't like the idea of the archdiocese giving this parish to a religious community. I had seen that happen to a lot of inner city parishes and I simply didn't like the idea. I figured that this kind of parish would be a place where there would be lots of vocations to the priesthood and I didn't want all those vocations going to the Franciscans or Salesians or Dominicans or whatever. We needed the vocations for the archdiocese. Otherwise, I'd end up being an old padre with nobody to help me run a parish.

So, I wrote to Wilton and told him I wanted to be the pastor. He said that I should wait a while and see how things went. He wanted to give me an out in case I couldn't take it physically, I guess. A few months later, he agreed to my request and I was named pastor of Immaculate Conception Parish.

One spring afternoon around the time I was made pastor, I was standing outside in front of the church. A bunch of kids from Houston Avenue came running toward the corner of 88th and Commercial. Another bunch came from Escanaba. They were going to meet and shoot at each other on the very corner where I was standing. This was a pretty frequent scenario, I had already found out, and the police usually arrived long after the shooting had stopped. There was also a lady with a stroller on the corner. As soon as the first shots rang out, she grabbed her baby and ran up the stairs of the church. She stood there screaming and pulling on the locked doors until I got up there and unlocked them.

The shooters disappeared almost immediately and I went back outside with her. She was crying and thanking me for being there. Afterward, I noticed a bullet hole in one of the church doors and another one in the stained glass above the main entrance door.

I said to myself, "Something's got to be done about this bullshit." I was angry, young, and a little foolhardy. I didn't want any ladies with babies caught in the crossfire, so I came up with a plan. I put on my "padre clothes" and went to have a little talk with the gangs. They each had their particular corner, and it wasn't too hard to find them. I brought along a whistle, the kind a gym teacher uses. In my conversations with each of the rival gangs, I made sure to tell them: "You aren't allowed to shoot at each other in front of my church any more. If I hear you starting up, I'm going to run out there in between the two groups and blow my whistle."

The prelude to shooting around here is usually that two groups start shouting at each other. They shout gang slogans, working themselves up to pulling the trigger, and then the shooting starts. I figured I'd have time to get between the groups if I moved as soon as the shouting started. I told each gang, "You'll have to choose. You know you have bad aim. If you shoot, you might hit me, and you'll go to hell for it." I knew from my experience with gangs that they would never intentionally shoot at a padre.

A couple of weeks later, I was sitting in my office and I heard some shouting...kids cranking themselves up to be brave. I looked over toward Commercial, got my whistle, and went outside. Sure enough, there were kids on Commercial and some other kids on Houston. I positioned myself between the groups and started yelling at them to go home. A woman who lived on the corner of 88th and Houston was watching all this from her back porch.

I yelled out to her, "Call the cops!"

"I can't. I'm afraid," she answered.

"CALL THE COPS!" I repeated.

She just stood there, shaking.

I shouted, "I'll come in and call them."

She said okay, and so I ran over and went into the house. As soon as I got out of the way, the shots started. I called 911 and told the operator, "I'm a Catholic priest. I was standing between these two groups and they weren't shooting. I came in here to call you and they've started shooting. Do you hear it?"

I held the phone up to the open window so she could hear the gunfire.

"I'm going back out there. If I get killed, it'll look really bad for the police."

I hung up the phone and ran back outside. As soon as I got there, the shooting stopped again.

Within seconds, the police were there. They arrived as if they were invading Grenada, swarming all over the place and coming from all directions. The whole situation was defused in a couple of minutes.

I went back to the rectory, had a glass of lemonade, and tried to calm my nerves. There was a fly trapped by the screen in my kitchen window. I opened the window and let him out. I didn't feel like killing anything that day.

If you're a reasonably sane person, you might wonder why I would stand between two groups of people with guns who are shooting at each other. I used to laughingly explain this kind of behavior by saying I was lazy. I would tell people that it was easier for me to stop someone from getting killed than it was to bury them. There's all the work of going to the wake, celebrating the funeral Mass, going to the cemetery, and all the rest.

The fact is that I would much rather prevent someone getting killed than bury them. Over the past eighteen years I've buried more gang shooting victims than I can remember, and I hate it. You might think it gets easier, that a person would get used to it all and not be bothered. In fact, the opposite is true. It seems to get more difficult as time goes by. Maybe it's because I think too much. I keep turning over the whole situation in my head—the neighborhood, the kids, their families, the injustice of it all. I guess you never really get used to evil.

I used to tell people that I wanted to save myself the work of burying these kids. I don't say that anymore. The truth is, they're kids. They don't really have a clue about what adult life is like, and they have weapons. They would never intentionally shoot a padre. Never.

These kids ... they have a real hunger for spirituality. If you give them half a chance and take them out of danger, their spirits come alive. The human spirit is remarkably resilient.

The Latin Kings Meet the Trappists

I had been going on silent retreats for a few years when it occurred to me that some of the gang kids I'd gotten to know might want to go on a silent retreat. I didn't think it was too crazy an idea at the time, taking a group of Latin Kings over to New Melleray Abbey in Iowa.

It didn't take me too long to talk a few of the guys into going on a retreat. It probably had to do with the fact that they knew me, and they wanted to get out of the neighborhood for a few days. Even though I told them they couldn't talk for a week, they still said that they wanted to go.

On the Monday morning we were to leave, I went in the van I'd borrowed and got the boys. A few of them had been up pretty much all night. They were carrying their clothes in those plastic bags you get when you buy your groceries. On the way out to the abbey, I reminded them that we were going to a retreat house, that they were expected to be quiet, that we would have plenty to eat, and that it should be a good time for them all. A couple of them fell asleep in the back of the van and we had a quiet ride out to the Trappist monastery.

After a few hours on the expressway we arrived at New Melleray. Trappist monks are famous for a few things. They don't talk. They don't eat meat. They offer wonderful hospitality. And they are happy!

The guest master met us in the reception area and told me what rooms the guys were assigned to. There were six of us all together, so he'd put us into adjoining rooms on the second floor of the "hospital." That's what they call the guest quarters;

the connection is to the word "hospitality," because people go there to get well. The whole abbey was made of limestone and had the solid feel of something meant to last forever. The quality of the silence in the halls impressed even these teenagers and they instinctively began to whisper as we walked to our assigned rooms.

The guys looked at their rooms and I think they were impressed. They each had a bathroom and a twin bed. These were the largest and cleanest rooms the guys had ever slept in, I think. As they took it all in, they didn't say much.

We went downstairs and found the cookie jar in the guest area. I told them they were certainly not to speak in the house, since they might bother the other guests, and then I suggested that we go for a walk. The Trappists have a big farm with lots of woods around. I knew these guys would like going for a walk, especially at night, and I wanted to show them where the path was while it was still daylight. I told them they were not allowed to go into the enclosure of the monastery (that's the back part that's closed to the public) and we took off to find the path through the woods.

We walked a short distance, past the nearby Lutheran church. The guys were fascinated with the graveyard...and I suspected they'd probably go back at night. We walked across the road and into the cornfields, where the monks had set up a little area with a few pine trees on top of a hill for quiet reflection. Then I told them I'd see them at dinner at 5:30 and headed back for a little rest. I was already getting pretty stressed out, thinking I must have been out of my mind for having brought these kids here.

They showed up early for dinner, and we went down and ate in silence. The guys were happy and horsing around a little, even though they didn't talk during the meal. After dinner we went to the chapel and watched as the monks prayed Compline, the last of the monastic prayers for the day. The guys were impressed by the solemnity and prayerfulness of it all.

The chapel has no ornamentation. It's very simple and extraordinarily beautiful, with limestone walls that go up forever. Outsiders gather at the far end of the chapel to pray with the monks. Compline concludes with the *Salve Regina*, an ancient Latin song. While it's being sung, the lights are turned off and the one light that shines on the icon of the Virgin is gradually dimmed until darkness envelops the chapel. Even the devil must get tears in his eyes when he hears this song.

After Compline, the guys want to go for a walk. I tell them the door gets locked at 9:00 and they must be in by then or they'll have to wake up the guest master and that won't be good. When they go off for their walk, I stay to pray and read for a while. Darkness falls, and with it a sense of tremendous peace and prayerfulness comes over the monastery. I decide to go and sit in the Adirondack chairs that are set up on the front lawn.

About a half an hour after dark, I hear noise coming from the entrance driveway. I can't see a thing, since when it's dark in the country, it's dark. Finally, I make out the shapes of the guys coming down the driveway. They're walking very slowly toward the monastery. Every once in a while I hear a strange sound coming from off on the side somewhere. Then they all scream and start laughing. I'm thinking of all the other guests and worried that the monks are going to send us home for bothering other people. I go walking down the driveway in that purposeful way you walk when you're going to deliver bad news. I approach the guys.

"You guys are making way too much noise. You're going to keep all the other guests up all night. What's the matter with you?" My stage-whisper voice has a hard edge to it. They don't say much back.

"What are you doing, anyway?"

Juventino, the only kid who's not in a gang, speaks up.

"We went over to that church over there." He points to the Lutheran church.

"There's a graveyard in the back."

Lucky starts talking. "Yeah, it was cool. Then it started getting dark. And we didn't want to get lost. And it was scary, too."

Then Beto jumps in. "So we started coming back. And I walked slower than the rest of them. And they got ahead of me. Then I went off on the side and scared them. 'Booooo.' They jumped and then I ran back close to them."

"We were taking turns scaring each other," Lefty says, "and we were getting real scared."

"Well, you guys are making way too much noise. This whole place is full of people who need to rest. And you little assholes are ruining it for them." I was way too cranked up for the situation. They looked at me as if I'd killed one of them, and I still didn't get it. I went on, "You're going to have to calm down." By now they were all serious and quiet. "If anybody can't be quiet around the house, they can just tell me, and we'll put them on the bus home tomorrow morning."

"I want to go." Lucky was looking at the ground. "I don't like it here."

I finally got it. I'd gone too far. I was amazed. These were some tough kids. Kids who'd been through all kinds of hell. Kids who'd probably shot at someone. Now, faced with a little yelling, they were ready to fold up. I told Lucky that he and I would talk after everyone had gone to bed.

"I didn't mean to offend you," I said to Lucky after the other guys had gone to their rooms.

"Uh-huh."

"I'm sorry."

"'Atts okay. I just wanna go home."

"Why?"

"I don't like it here."

"Why don't you give it a few days?"

"What's the use?"

"What do you mean, what's the use?"

"What's the use? We'll just go back to where we came from. This isn't real."

"Yes it is. It's real. It's more real than hanging around on a corner worrying that someone is going to kill you."

Lucky just sat there. Somehow we started a conversation that lasted most of the night. As we talked, Lucky told me his father had said to him more than once, "I wish you had never been born." He cried a little when he told me that. We talked and talked and I told him that, if he still wanted to go home in the morning, I'd put him on the Greyhound back to Chicago.

During the course of the night, I learned that these guys were more delicate than your normal kids when it came to a man yelling at them. A woman could scream her lungs out at them and it would be okay. That would seem normal to them, like their mothers yelling at them. They just couldn't take masculine disapproval.

Lucky decided to stay.

Tuesday morning I met with the guest master and asked him if he'd do us the favor of finding some physical work for the guys. The Trappists have always extended me this kindness, the opportunity to do some work. It's almost impossible to spend the whole day in contemplative prayer, especially when you've been involved in an active life. I knew the guys would need some work, too.

The guest master told me they didn't have anything in particular that day, but that the Trappistines did. They're lady Trappists, and their monastery isn't too far from the abbey at New Melleray. I was also eager for the guys to meet one of the sisters in particular, because she used to be in a gang in Chicago.

We went off, and the guys were fascinated by the place. It wasn't as impressive as the abbey where the monks lived and worked, but it seemed more inviting. Maybe it was just the feminine presence, but the guys immediately took to the place and the nuns.

Our Lady of the Mississippi Abbey spreads out over the high bluffs on the western bank of the river. The nuns were very welcoming. They gave us lemonade and invited us all for a little tour. The guys got to talk to the ex–gang member and were duly impressed!

Then we went to work picking grapes. These guys weren't used to hard physical work and groused a little about it at first. Then they saw that the women were working harder than they were and were embarrassed into putting some effort into it. I remember the intense smell of the grapes and the kids being afraid of the bees and the sun beating down on us and the sweat and the glasses of cold lemonade. It was a wonderful afternoon working in the sun. When the guys were asked if they could come back the next day to help bail hay, they responded with great enthusiasm. They wanted to stay with these cloistered nuns and were disappointed to find that there wasn't room enough to move into their guest quarters.

Tuesday night back with the Trappists, nothing much happened. After Compline and the guys went off to their rooms. I stayed awake reading and praying for a while. Then, at around 10:00, I decided to go and make sure that they were all in their rooms. I knocked on the first of the doors and got no answer. I knocked a little more loudly, then opened the door. No kid.

Now I'm thinking, "They're off somewhere, breaking stuff or doing who knows what." I knock on the second door. No answer. I open the door. No kid. I go down the hall, quietly knocking on all the doors and finding no one. By now I am getting really nervous. "Where could they be?"

Finally, I knock on the last door. I hear small sounds coming out of the room and open the door. There are three kids in the bed and two on the floor. "What are you doing in here?"

"We couldn't sleep."

"What?"

"We got scared. We couldn't sleep."

"You mean to tell me that each of you has his own room, his own bathroom, his own door, and you don't want them?"

"Yeah. We like it better in here together."

I had an executive decision to make. Was I going to push this one?

"All right. Fine. Just don't make any noise."

"Did you hear us before?"

"No."

"We won't make any noise. We promise."

"And don't stay up talking all night either. We have to be up early tomorrow to go help the nuns."

"We know."

On Wednesday morning we got up at 6:00 and went to breakfast. Then we headed to Our Lady of the Mississippi. The Trappistines had been up for hours already and wanted help bailing hay. These guys had never so much as seen a hay bailer, but they got the hang of it pretty quickly. The tractor drives through the field, cutting the hay and making bales. It spits each bale out a chute in the back. Someone catches the bale and tosses it to the next person, who stacks it on the back of the wagon being pulled by the tractor. The bales weigh about sixty-five pounds and throwing them around is hard work.

The guys took to it like fish to water. Every once in a while, one of the older nuns would come out with some cold lemonade. The guys felt like they were making a difference. They were doing physical work and they loved it. And the nuns were very kind. Very hard working, and very kind.

In the afternoon, we headed back to New Melleray. I was pretty shot after all the worry and work, and so I decided I'd have a little rest. I told the boys I'd see them at 4:30. After a little rest and prayer, I went down to the entrance to meet the boys. The only one there was Juventino.

"Where are the rest of the guys?"

"I don't know." He wouldn't look at me. I knew something was up.

"Where do you think they are?"

"I don't know."

"I know you don't know. Where do you think they are?"

He sat there on the steps, quiet. Then he answered.

"I think they took a car."

"What?"

"I think they took a car. I saw a blue car over there," he pointed to where the visitors to the chapel would park.

"It had the keys in it, and now it's gone. And I haven't seen Lucky or Beto or anyone."

Oh shit. That's what I thought. These Iowa people still leave the keys in their cars when they go somewhere. I began to imagine Lucky and Beto riding across cornfields in someone's Chevy. I walked down to the parking area with Juventino and asked him were the car had been parked. He pointed to the spot.

What could I do? I went back to the steps and sat there with Juventino. I wanted to cry, thinking about these guys stealing a car and some poor farmer or farmer's wife finding their car gone and wrecked. We sat there for around twenty minutes.

Then I heard a noise behind me. There was Lucky and, right behind him, Beto. Their hair was all standing up.

"Where have you been?" They didn't realize I had been imagining them wrapped around a tree somewhere.

"We were tired. So we were sleeping."

"Oh." Thank God, I thought. Thank God. Still, the stress was killing me!

The guys were getting into the habit of going to Compline and then going back to their rooms afterward. I decided that maybe we'd try getting together after Compline, so we got a few of the Adirondack chairs and made a little circle in the grass in front of the abbey. We spent a couple of hours talking about different things. I learned that what the gang members had in common was the fact that all their fathers had told them they wished their sons had never been born. I was deeply saddened . . .

When the sun went down, I reminded the boys that we had work to do the next day.

Thursday morning we got up at 6:00 and went to breakfast. One of the monks brought out some special bread and gave it to the boys. He smiled and said, "Those Trappistines will work you to death. Take this and have some during the day if you get hungry." It was as if someone had given these guys a million bucks.

We arrived over at Our Lady of the Mississippi and it was "box delivery day." The main source of income for the Trappistines is homemade candies, and they get a semi-trailer full of boxes once in a while. This was the day to unload the semi! The boys spent the whole morning working and sweating and drinking glasses of lemonade. They felt like they were in heaven.

That night after Compline we sat on the lawn again and just talked about life. It was a new experience for them, working hard and being physically tired at the end of the day. New to them was the idea that they could work together, sleep soundly, and wake up early. Also new was the experience of sitting outside as dusk fell and talking about life. It was the kind of wholesome rhythm of life and work and rest that the Trappists had found centuries ago. They loved it.

On Friday the Trappistines didn't have any work for us, but the Trappists did. The guest master told me he wanted us to paint a barn. We went into the enclosure and the guys were pie-eyed, looking at the huge vegetable garden and all the monastery buildings they hadn't yet seen. The monk in charge of painting gave each of us coveralls and a paintbrush.

Then he gave us the paint and pointed us toward a beat-up old flatbed truck. "You can use that as a scaffold," he said. "Tell the guys to get on and we'll drive over to the barn."

The boys piled on the back of the truck and off we went across the fields. We arrived at an old, old barn and parked alongside it. The monk got out of the truck and said, "Okay. I guess you know what to do."

I watched him walk away and then I turned back to the guys. "All right. Lucky, you and Juventino take that side." I pointed to one side of the barn. "Start from the top and paint your way to the bottom."

I put two on another side and had one work with me on the west side of the barn. Everything was going along fine, and I heard the usual chatter that goes along with kids being together. Then things got quiet. Too quiet.

I walked around to the south side of the barn and there it was. I should have been prepared for this. Give a gangbanger a paintbrush and what can you expect? Graffiti. This was the biggest "L K" I'd ever seen. The letters were easily ten feet tall and the guys were smirking and looking at me to see my reaction. Of course, they got what they were looking for.

"You assholes. Get that shit offa there before the monks see it. Get painting. Quick. Before someone sees. All of you paint on this side where I can see you."

This time they were unimpressed by my cursing and were actually laughing as they painted out the letters. After a while, I went around to the other side of the barn with one of the guys to keep working. All of a sudden, I saw Lucky running away and cursing. "You motherfucker!" he shouted as he turned around and dipped his paint brush into his can. "There, take that!"—and he sprayed the other guy with barn paint.

"Oh yeah!" I heard from around the corner of the barn, "How do you like this?"—and paint sprayed back at Lucky.

By the time I got around the corner, it was a free-for-all. All of the guys were splashing each other with paint and laughing and laughing.

"You fuckers. Stop that! Look, you're getting paint all over everything. And yourselves too. Stop it!" They stopped, but they were still laughing.

"Get back to work. I don't know what I'm going to tell the monks about their coveralls. Just look at this shit."

At that moment, one of the monks came walking up. He was tall and thin and had gray hair. He had heard me and he said, "When you take these coveralls off, they're going to say: 'Take off your clothes and step behind the yellow line. Nobody cross the line.'"

The kids looked at him in amazement. I did, too. I knew those words from having taught Bible classes at Cook County Jail. Where could he know them from?

"Where did you learn that?" Lucky asked him.

"I been around," the monk answered, with a small smile.

"You been in jail?"

"Yep."

Then he started the guys working on the side of the barn. They worked quietly and once in a while they asked him a question. They were amazed that he was talking to them.

Meantime, Lucky couldn't resist, so he snuck off and graffitied the side of the truck...or maybe he'd done it before. In any case, when I went to move the truck to paint a different part of the barn, I saw "L K" painted on the window of the truck and on the door. By now, my patience was wearing thin.

"Lucky. Come over here and get this OFF the truck."

He came over with a rag and some paint thinner and got most of the graffiti off the truck. We finished up painting and went back to return our coveralls. The monk in charge of paint, clothes, etc. didn't say anything as we handed in the stuff. I apologized for returning the clothes in such bad shape.

We went back to take showers, rest, and eat dinner. That night, we spent a couple of hours on the front lawn of the monastery talking about life again.

On Saturday morning, I had to meet with the guest master to explain the graffiti on the truck and apologize for all the other disturbances the guys had caused. I was pretty mortified, thinking of what his reaction might be. I began to explain,

"I'm really sorry about the truck..."

"What?"

"The truck, and the coveralls, and all the mess we made painting..."

"What mess?"

"Well, the guys were painting, and they started painting each other, and the paint got all over the coveralls and the truck and they graffitied the truck and all that..."

"Oh that. We had a great laugh last night about that. Brother Luke was telling us about all the paint and the truck and the barn. We really enjoyed his story."

I sat there shocked.

"That always happens. We always send the novices to paint that same barn. They come back with more paint on themselves than on the barn," he told me laughing. "We think they have a great time painting each other."

The monks had seen what I had missed. These were kids playing, not gangbangers doing destruction. I guess that's the advantage of holiness. You can see much more clearly.

I went back to tell the guys to pack up and get ready to go. They were moving pretty slowly.

"Can we stay?" Beto asked me as we walked down the hallway to leave.

"No. You have to go back home."

"Oh."

"Maybe someday you can come back here to live and be a monk."

"That would be good."

We went back to Chicago. Two days after we got there, Lucky was shot. A couple of days after that, Beto ended up in the county jail. Still, it had been a great trip.

I hope one of them will remember the Trappists sometime and actually believe there's a place to go where nobody wants to kill you.

After this experience, I began to see gangs and gang members in a completely different light. In the end, they're kids. I truly believe that no one ever makes a choice they perceive to be bad for them. Each of us weighs the pros and cons of our decisions and chooses what we think is best for us. Unfortunately, for these kids, the pros and cons end up leading them to join a gang. It's the best choice they can make for themselves.

Maybe someday we'll come up with a way to change that for these kids. Maybe not. The evil involved in creating a situation where the best choice is to become a gang member is pretty intense.

I may be a little crazy, but I am not afraid of the gangs that ring Immaculate Conception. They all know me, and they also know that I mean them no harm. They realize that someday I may have to comfort their families or visit them in jail. They would never intentionally shoot me. The advantage I have is that people know me as the priest, and I'm easily recognizable, being a white guy and all. Not everyone shares that advantage. Pity the poor seminarians who came to work here!

Negro Orders from Capri's

I had arrived in the parish in January, and the place needed some fixing up. The office where I worked had been remodeled in the 1970s, when there was an energy scare and the parish still had some money. The renovations involved taking twelve-foot ceilings down to eight feet, cutting off the top half of the office windows, putting up formica paneling on the walls and ceiling, and generally making a beautiful space ugly. With the shag indoor/outdoor carpet on the floor, the place was more suited for a livestock pen than for a pastor's office.

Some of the seminarians I'd gotten to know in my former parish volunteered to come and spend the summer fixing the place up. I was happy for the help, and for the company. They arrived during the first week of June.

Unfortunately, I was due to go on a two-week vacation right after their arrival. I knew they would be okay, though, because Zeke Sanchez was one of the seminarians. He was solid as a rock and handy with a paint roller. I left them some tools and paint and took off for my two weeks on Monday morning.

That Monday evening at around 10:00 they heard some shouting in front of the rectory. Zeke was the oldest, and the one in charge. He later told me that they had been standing at the upstairs windows and Zeke warned them to step back. He'd been in this kind of neighborhood before and he knew what might happen. Sure enough, across the street a guy was shot.

One of the seminarians, Negro, was deeply shocked. He had never seen anything like this before. (I guess I should let you know that, among Mexicans, having dark skin or light skin is generally no big deal. In the same family, one brother can have really light skin and blue eyes and another brother dark skin and brown eyes. So, "Negro"—Spanish for "black"—was this young man's nickname.)

The seminarians called the police. The cops arrived after a few minutes, followed by the paramedics who took the wounded man away. The seminarians watched all this from the upstairs windows.

I arrived back after my two weeks away and wanted to see what they'd accomplished. But what they wanted was to tell me about the shooting. So we sat down together and they gave me a detailed account of what had happened. It turned out that they hadn't gotten much done in my absence!

In fact, Negro hadn't left the rectory for the whole two weeks I was away. If he got hungry, he ordered a pizza from Capri's, the place around the corner, and had it delivered! He was too afraid to even leave the house. The other guys mocked him mercilessly, calling him a little girl. Negro came from a peaceful neighborhood and had never seen anyone shot. He was also "unknown" and not a white guy. He might have been mistaken for a gang member. Being white, I'm actually a lot safer than the young guys who've come to the parish to work.

After years of dealing with Hispanic seminarians, I've figured it out. Most people who see me walking around the neighborhood think I'm either a cop or an immigration officer, or they know I'm the priest. The young Hispanic seminarians don't enjoy the same protections. They feel safe walking around with me, but terribly threatened walking alone.

The same is true for any of the young guys who live in or around the neighborhood. It's a pretty regular thing, I've found, for these guys to have people wave guns at them, to call out gang slogans, shouting KING LOVE as they walk by, for example, to threaten them, to actually shoot at them. They achieve some measure of safety by paying close attention to their environment, by being always vigilant and watching for signs of impending gang battles, by avoiding "dangerous houses," and by learning absolutely the "lay of the land." They sometimes walk a zigzag around bad blocks to get to school, making what should be a ten-minute walk into a half-hour trek. Their parents usually don't know about these long daily detours.

And these are the good guys, the ones who come to Mass every Sunday, the ones who try to do their homework, the ones who are part of the youth group in the parish, the ones who are trying to make a life. Even so, the reality of living here means that they might be killed at any moment, on their front porch, in their beds as they sleep, or going to Capri's to get a pizza.

When I get tempted to feel sorry for myself, I remember the "safety features" of my life that are not built into the lives of these young people. I'm white. I'm a priest. I can walk away at any time and go work somewhere much less dangerous. And—perhaps most important of all—I have a brick house. Thank God for the old-timers who put the place up. Bullets don't go through bricks. I've set up my bed far enough away from the windows that a bullet could never hit me while I'm sleeping. There's a bullet hole in the screen of my bedroom window, but I've checked the angles and there's no way I could get shot in bed. The dining room of the house has had the windows shot out a few times, but we've replaced the glass and gone on. Thank God nobody has been in the room when the windows were being shot out. The people in the house across the street aren't as lucky. One night while they were asleep in the corner bedroom, a bullet came flying through one wall, over the bed, and out the other wall. They have a frame house.

Raul Saves His Kitchen Cabinets

When I arrived in South Chicago, the house right across the street from the rectory was abandoned. So was the one on the opposite corner. The drug guys were using both houses for sales, and the prostitutes found them handy, too. Maybe that's why the guy got shot there when Negro and Zeke and the guys came for the summer. Abandoned buildings tend to attract problems.

Then Neighborhood Housing Services decided that our neighborhood was a good place to start working, and they began lending people money to fix up buildings. Everyone in Chicago wants a brick house. You can see why. These two buildings were good candidates for rehab because they were made of brick and stood on corners.

So, I met Raul. He's a little Mexican guy who bought the abandoned building across the street. It was a good deal, a brick two-flat for a song. I'd see him there every day after work, doing something or another on the building. He'd be working on the yard, or cleaning out the garage, or whatever. He never stopped working, and it was a good thing. The building had to be completely gutted, the plaster torn off the walls and the junk cleared out. Around here, buildings that are empty invite scavengers. Guys will come in at night and pretty well clean out the building. They'll use sledgehammers to break up the radiators, which they throw out the windows and load on their pickups to sell for scrap. They'll take all the copper pipes, all the regular pipes, the sinks and toilets, the wires out of the walls, and pretty much whatever they can get out of

49

the house. So, by the time Raul got title for the building, there was almost nothing left on the inside.

The rehabbers knocked all the plaster down and took it away. They put in new windows and were working on conduit for the wires when Raul got robbed the first time. He called me over one afternoon, "Come over, Padre, and have a look at this." I went across the street and saw that someone had taken a hammer to his new glass block window. They'd gotten into the house and taken all the tools and the wire from the electrician. He was pretty mad, and with good reason, so he quit the next day.

Raul had a very hard time finding another electrician, since nobody wanted to come and work in South Chicago. Finally, though, he managed to find one, and the job moved along. Workers came and put in the drywall, and the plumbing was nearly completed.

Then he was robbed the second time. This time they got all the kitchen cabinets. Raul brought me over and pointed to the empty kitchen wall. "Those damn cabinets cost a fortune. I'm going to sleep here from now on, Padre. I'll get a little fold-up cot and sleep right here," he told me.

He went and got a replacement set of kitchen cabinets, and the job was once again moving forward. Raul slept in the kitchen at night and worked as a laborer during the day.

A couple of days later, he called me over again. "Come and look, Padre." I went across the street. He was pretty happy. He invited me into the house, into the kitchen where he had his little cot set up. "Last night they were coming in here again."

I nodded.

"Thieves are like dogs," he said. "Once they start pissing in a place, it's hard to get them to stop."

I nodded again.

"So," he continued, "last night I was sleeping right here. I heard a sound on the back porch and that woke me up. Then I heard them start banging on the glass blocks right over there."

He pointed to the glass blocks a few feet away. "I grabbed my gun, said a prayer to the Virgin Mary that I'd miss them, then I shot the wall, right here." He pointed to a bullet hole in the wall, right next to the glass blocks. "They ran down the steps, and I rushed over to the back door. I opened the door, said another prayer to the Virgin, and fired one more shot over their heads. I yelled at them and called them motherfuckers. They went around the corner and started running down the alley. I said another prayer to the Virgin that I'd miss them, yelled at them again, and fired a final shot over their heads. They won't be coming back here any more."

Raul was pretty happy telling me all this, but he could see from the the look on my face that I was a little taken aback by what he was saying. Here was this really nice guy, this hardworking guy, this guy who came to Mass every Sunday, shooting at people.

He tried to explain. "I really didn't want to hit anyone. Imagine how I'd feel, knowing I had actually shot a person. That's why I prayed to the Virgin, begging her that I wouldn't hit anyone."

I smiled and shook my head back and forth.

"I never seen a thief move so fast in all my life," he told me. Then he laughed and said again, "They won't be coming back here any more!"

Some Guys Looking for a Spare Tire

It was around 6:00 on a summer Sunday morning. Raul had moved into his recently rehabbed house and the world was at peace. It was promising to be a hot day—already it was really warm. I was sitting in the kitchen in my gym shorts and tee shirt, having a cup of coffee and thinking/praying about what to say about the Gospel at Mass later in the day.

I heard some guys talking on the corner opposite the rectory and looked over to see what was up. You do that in the city. You try to watch other people's stuff. Raul had been keeping an eye on the rectory, and I was just returning the favor. There were three guys there, having a little conference across the street from Raul's house. They looked to be in their mid-twenties and were taking the tenuous steps of people who've been partying all night and think the sunshine is too bright.

Two of the guys started heading over to a car parked on 88th Street. They were carrying a tire iron. I thought they might be going to break a window. My curiosity was piqued, so I stood up with my coffee cup in my hand and watched them approach the car. No. They weren't going to break the window. They were going to take a tire. They didn't even jack up the car. They just loosened the lug bolts and pulled. The car fell down and they pulled the tire loose from the wheel well.

I got a little aggravated, thinking the car might be Arturo's from across the street, or maybe Raul's, or maybe some other neighbor's. I thought about calling the police, but gave up on the idea. If they don't come when there's shooting, why would they come when somebody's stealing a tire?

The guys tried the tire on their own car and it didn't fit. As they stood there staring at their flat, they must have decided to try and find another Ford so that they could get a tire that would fit. Two of them set off down the block with the tire iron. That left one standing on the corner, probably looking out in case a cop came down the street.

I make up my mind to go over and talk to the guy. Turning away from the window, I call the dog and say, "Wanna go for a walk?" He responds as he usually does to the sight of his leash. What joy!

We go outside and walk up to the guy standing on the corner. He's a lot bigger than I am, and a lot younger, but I have the Duke on a leash. As we approach, the guy eyes the dog. The Duke is 115 pounds of love (what other kind of dog could you have in a rectory?), but he's kind of ugly. I stand on the corner and the dog strains on the leash. The guy doesn't know that the Duke wants to lick him to death, so he's a little on the defensive. I tell the dog to sit—and, for once, he does!

"Hello."

The guy looks at me with ice in his eyes. He doesn't answer, but he shifts his weight and adopts the "I'm about to take a swing at you" stance. I ignore this. I don't know what he thinks of me, a white guy outside at 6:30 on a Sunday morning dressed in gym shorts and a tee shirt with a big dog. It doesn't matter. He aggravates me.

"You guys been taking tires?"

The guy's look gets harder. "What's it to you?"

"Well, that car over there might be Raul's. He's got to go to work. How do you think he'll feel when he comes out and the tire's gone?"

The guy doesn't even pause to think.

"How do you think you'll feel if I kill you?" He says this while looking me right in the eye.

By now his two buddies have returned empty-handed from their trip down the block with the tire iron. Maybe their heads are really pounding. Maybe the big guy I'm talking to is hung over, or still high. I don't know. Somehow this has gotten ugly, but still, it's just not right. So I answer the guy, "I'd be dead. But it's still wrong to steal people's tires."

He stands there looking at me for an awfully long time. I'm thinking he's debating whether to kill me or not. I wonder if the dog will stick up for me.

Finally his buddy speaks. "Ahh. Let's just go."

They walk away. I go back to getting ready for Sunday Mass. It's mighty hard to concentrate on today's Gospel right now. Still, you have to watch your neighbor's stuff.

There's a fly sitting on my desk as I'm trying to prepare my sermon for Mass. I shoo it off and get back to work.

The Nigerian Gets a Scare

There's a Nigerian resident living in the rectory. His name is Fr. Tony. He's studying at Catholic Theological Union, getting a doctorate in ministry. He's also working as a chaplain at Little Company of Mary hospital. He and I have talked about the shooting around here, and he seems to have made peace with the gunfire. He says that the fact that he was a chaplain for the army in Nigeria is a big help. He's used to the sound of gunfire.

One day, Tony invited another Nigerian, Fr. John, over for dinner. John had never worked in a neighborhood like this one. It was a warm summer evening, and they were standing out in front by John's car. Suddenly, they heard a popping noise from what sounded like a few blocks away. John asked, "What's that?"

Tony didn't want to scare him, so he answered, "It's firecrackers."

They stood there talking for a little while longer. The sounds got louder.

"Are you sure it's firecrackers?"

"Yes, don't worry about it."

As he was speaking, a kid who was about twelve years old came riding up on a bicycle and stopped in the middle of the intersection of 88th and Exchange, maybe a car-length from where the two of them were standing. The gangs usually have the "shorties" do the shooting, since even if they get caught they won't face adult charges. The kid planted his feet on either side of the bike frame, pulled out a gun, and started shooting down the block. After firing a few shots, he took off down 88th, away from the two padres.

John was speechless. He'd never seen anything even remotely like what he'd just witnessed. He said, "I'll see you later," jumped into his car, and drove away. When Tony told me later about what had happened, we both laughed.

John doesn't come here any more. A lot of people get shaken up when they visit the parish. It's especially hard when strangers come from outside the neighborhood for big events, like confirmation.

Once a year we have confirmation here at the parish. It's an important day for us, and the bishop comes. The kids are all dressed up, parents and godparents fill the church, people arrive from out of town, and it's a pretty big deal.

Twice in the past six years there's been gunfire outside right near the end of the Mass. The ushers have learned what to do. They all have a key to the cabinet where we've put a phone for situations like this one. They call 911, report the incident, then one of them comes up to the front. He'll whisper in my ear, "Padre, they're shooting outside." Sometimes we can hear it in the church, if we're not singing a song at the time. If we're singing, the music drowns out the shooting. In any case, if I get the word, I get up and make an announcement:

"After Mass, please do not go outside. Instead, everyone is invited down to the parish hall for some refreshments and to meet the bishop. They're shooting out there right now. We'll tell you when it's safe to leave."

The regulars all know this is par for the course. It does tend to frighten the visitors, though.

Noe's Homework

The rectory is pretty much open to any kid who wants to come in and do homework. That way they can find a place to read and write, a place to concentrate without the distractions of brothers and sisters and cousins and television.

Not too long ago I found Noe doing his homework. He's an altar boy who lives across the street on the second floor of Raul's building. I looked at the page he was working on and saw columns of words, each one written ten times. One set of words read something like "spyre, spyre, spyre, spyre." A lot of the other words weren't English. I thought for a moment that the school might be teaching the kids French, or perhaps German. I didn't recognize one word until I came to "game." Then I thought perhaps the kids were being taught the "new spelling," where each student invents the spelling for a word. I asked Noe where he was getting these words.

He pulled a page from the bottom of the pile and showed it to me. It was a spelling test. Noe had gotten all of the words wrong and the teacher had assigned him homework of copying each word ten times. I saw that he had in fact written out the words ten times—but most of them were spelled incorrectly. Then I looked more closely at his test and realized that some of the words that were marked wrong had been spelled correctly in the first place.

I asked him again where he was getting these words from and whether he had a textbook. He told me that the teacher had the book and he didn't have a copy. I saw that the test paper had been stamped with a "Parent Signature Required" stamp. I wrote the correct spellings on the test next to the incorrect words and I put a "?" next to the ones spelled correctly. I also wondered what "Parent Signature Required" meant on a test paper when the parents do not read English. After I'd checked all the words for correct spelling, Noe went back to finishing his homework.

Then Beto came in with his results from the Archbishop Quigley High School Seminary entrance exam. Beto is one of the best students at Arnold Mireles Elementary School. His latest report card had been all "As," with one "B" in reading.

He was elated now, because he had been accepted into Quigley. He pulled out the sheet that came in the mail, summarizing his test results on a graph. I looked at the graph and then looked at his face beaming with joy. How could I tell him? According to the graph, he had scored in the 28th percentile. The 50th percentile is average. That meant that he had scored way below average.

I didn't tell him how he would have to struggle at Quigley just to keep his nose above water. I didn't tell him how he would have to work for three or four hours each night for at least two years just to survive in high school. Instead, I congratulated him on being accepted. And I remembered what had happened to his brother last year. He hadn't gotten in to Quigley.

Miguel and Popeye

On a Thursday afternoon last summer, Miguel and Popeye were walking on the sidewalk in front of the rectory. I wanted to catch up with Miguel, because I'd heard he was upset about not having been accepted into Quigley.

Archbishop Quigley is our high school seminary here in Chicago. They do a great job of working with kids from the neighborhood and encouraging vocations, so I try to send as many kids as I can from the parish. I'd wanted Miguel and Popeye to take the test, but Popeye had said, "Why bother? I won't get accepted anyway." I was angry at his response, but there was nothing I could do. Although Miguel did take the test, he didn't do well and didn't get accepted. Popeye probably would have passed the test...

When I caught up with the boys that day, I saw that Miguel was crying. I told him things would be all right anyway, and not to worry.

It's sad... these are guys with possible vocations to be priests, and they can't read well enough to get into our preparatory seminary. It's one of the reasons we decided to reopen our school, to give these kids half a chance.

Miguel and Popeye are pretty well inseparable, and they were walking down the sidewalk in front of the rectory that summer afternoon because they were on their way to feed hungry people. They both show up every Tuesday and Thursday to help out. This is in spite of the fact that their mothers are not too happy about their coming over. The moms get upset and worry because there is a lot of shooting on the streets. Their kids go out anyway—they tell their mothers that there are hungry people and they have to go and help them. I've found that happening a lot with young people. If you get them involved and they know they're doing something good, they'll keep doing it in spite of whatever it costs them.

That Thursday night, the youth group met. We were looking at the Gospel for Sunday. It was the one about Jesus getting a drink from a woman at a well. Then we heard a shot. It was from a big gun, too, maybe a shotgun. (Around here, you learn to distinguish the sounds of different kinds of guns.) "Boom!" Memo jumped up right away to look out the window. I was by the chalkboard in the dining room of the rectory. "Sit down, Memo," I yelled. Everybody wanted to go look out the window. I keep working on the Gospel.

Then there was another "Boom." This time it sounded like it was right outside the window. I ignored it and kept on going. Again, an even louder "BOOM." I said to Carlos, "Go and tell Saul to call the cops." Saul was the kid on the phones that night, and the kids usually know the drill. They hear shots and immediately call 911. Lately they've been taking to hiding under the desk while they dial.

I went back to working on the Gospel as if nothing had happened. The kids have to ask questions about the Gospel, and the one with the best question wins a prize. It's a method used in West Africa, and it works here, too. The best question today was, "Why did Jesus say to the Samaritan woman, 'You people worship what you do not understand'?" Jamie asked it and got the prize.

These kids have a real spiritual hunger. My sister-in-law recently asked me when I was going to work in a tough parish. I knew what she meant. Around here we're living in "biblical" territory. There are prostitutes and beggars and thieves and outcasts and beatings and death. It's easy to understand the Bible if you live in South Chicago. My sister-in-law thinks a parish somewhere in the suburbs would be tougher for me.

She's right. It's easy to preach the Gospel here where the evil is pretty well defined.

Someone once said that there are no atheists in foxholes. There are very few atheists in my neighborhood. Even the gang members know there's a God. I remember a guy named Ismael, who wanted to join the Church...

Ismael Joins the Catholic Church

We have a program in the parish called the RCIA (Rite of Christian Initiation for Adults). It's for people who want to become Catholic, whether they're wanting to be baptized, make their first communion, or be confirmed. We get a lot of teenagers who, for some reason or other, haven't received all the sacraments.

Ismael and Carlos came to join the RCIA. It turns out that they had not been baptized and their mom hadn't been able to put them in the religious education program when they were little. They were still young enough to obey their mother when she decided to send them to the parish for religious instruction. Ismael was the older brother, and Carlos younger.

During the year, they missed a few of the sessions and I went over to their house to see what was up. Their mother wasn't an active Catholic, but still, the guys had been coming to the sessions. They lived over on Escanaba, two short blocks from the church. Escanaba was (and is) Dragons territory.

When I visited and had a little talk with their mom, she promised they'd be more regular in coming on Sundays. They started appearing more frequently at the sessions and they were doing pretty well, learning all the "Catholic stuff."

At different points in the RCIA process, the catechists get together and look at the progress of the people in the program. Connie, one of the catechists, told me she didn't think Ismael should receive the sacraments because she'd heard he had joined the Latin Kings. She asked me to check out the story and decide what should be done.

It was one of those beautiful mornings we get in Chicago in the early spring. The sun was shining, the air had that smell of worms that means spring is coming, and it was warm enough to sit on the steps of the rectory and have a smoke between Sunday Masses. I caught sight of Ismael and Carlos as they were heading home and called Ismael over.

"Ismael, Connie tells me you're a Latin King."

He squirmed for a minute and didn't answer.

"Is it true?"

After a little more squirming, he answered,

"Yes."

I looked over at his little brother standing there and motioned to him with my head, "Do you think this is a good example for your little brother?"

"No," he said, as he hung his head.

"Why did you do it?"

After a pause he answered, "The Dragons wouldn't leave us alone. They were always starting something. At school, on the way there, on the way home. They wouldn't leave us alone."

I could see that he wanted to protect himself and his little brother. Still, he couldn't be a gangbanger and a Catholic at the same time. I wondered what to tell him. If he left the Kings, he would get a violation. The gang members would all get together and beat him up. Then they would no longer protect him. And the Dragons would still want to kill him.

"Ismael, you have to drop to become Catholic. You can't be a King and a Catholic at the same time."

He stood there looking at the ground for a while.

"What about all those Kings who go to Mass?"

"They're already Catholics . . . and they're not very good ones either."

"Yeah, but still, every Sunday there's a bunch of gangbangers at Mass."

I had to think about it for a minute.

"Still, you'll have to drop if you want to be a Catholic."

"Father Mike, do you have to be perfect to be a Catholic?" I had to think about that one for a while. I was beginning to waver. After all, isn't the Church full of sinners? Finally I answered him, "No, you don't have to be perfect. Still, you should drop."

"What about if something happens to me? How can I get to heaven if I'm not baptized?"

He won. What could I say?

"All right. All right. You can be baptized and receive the sacraments. Still, as soon as the school year is over, you have to drop. Is it a deal?"

"Yeah."

That Easter, Ismael and Carlos joined the Catholic Church.

I had hoped that they'd be coming to church regularly after Easter. I guess it was not meant to be. I kind of lost track of them both. . . . I'd see them occasionally on the street and say hello, but they were both getting more and more into the gangbanging lifestyle. That meant that they usually couldn't be hanging around outside too much. It would be too dangerous for them.

Stopped on Commercial

One summer afternoon after Ismael and Carlos had received the sacraments, I ran into them on Commercial, half a block from the church. It was a hot summer afternoon and I'd decided to take my little Honda scooter over to the street Mass I was going to celebrate. We'd been doing street Masses for a few years, scheduling a Mass every Saturday during the summer on different blocks, and it was my turn over on Baltimore. I was heading back after the Mass when it happened.

I'd pulled the scooter between a couple of parked cars and stopped to talk to some of the Latin Kings who were hanging out in front of the bakery. I had noticed Ismael in the group, and I wanted to see how he was and whether he'd given any more thought to leaving the Kings. I was sitting on the scooter between the cars when the police cars raced up and screeched to a stop right in the middle of the street. The cops leaped out of their car and shouted, "Okay, everybody put your hands on the trunk of the car!"

All the guys were used to this kind of stuff, and they didn't say anything. I didn't, either. I wanted to see how far these guys would push, violating my rights to stand and talk to people. I got off the scooter and put my hands on the trunk of a Chevy. I'd been harassed by the cops as a teenager and it didn't bother me too much.

The police asked the guys a few questions and there I stood. It was hot, and I was getting a little sweaty. I was the only white guy for blocks around, and here I was being rounded up with the gangbangers. People were stopping in the street and looking at us. Another police car arrived, and now this had turned into a major event on Commercial. Still, I stood there with my hands on the trunk and didn't say anything.

The windows of the second floor apartments above the stores on Commercial began to open, and people started sticking their heads out the windows. Somebody shouted from above, "Hey, you got the priest there!"

The cop in charge looked over at me, with my hands on the trunk, and then shouted to the lady in the window. "I give a shit if it's mother fuckin' Teresa. He's staying there."

I was shocked and angry, if the truth be told, and beginning to get a little afraid. I didn't say anything. I'd heard stories about coppers beating on people. I started thinking, "Shut up, lady. You'll only make it worse."

A different officer came over to me and asked me who I was. I told him I was the parish priest and I pointed half a block down to the church. Then I put my hand back on the trunk of the car. I stood there for a few minutes while he conferred with the guy in charge. Then they both came over and called me apart from the Latin Kings.

"Are you the priest?"

"Yes."

They had a hurried huddle, and after a few minutes of whispers came back to me. They called the guys over.

"Father, we got a deal for you. We won't take these guys in, if you'll agree to have a counseling session with them. They gotta go with you right now, or go to jail."

"Okay, officer. I'll talk to them."

We went down the block to the rectory and I had a little talk with them. When we were finished, I wanted to meet with Ismael alone. I asked the other guys to wait outside my office while I talked to Ismael. Among other things, I told him, "Ismael, you're a good guy. But you know what? You look like you're already dead. I can see it in your eyes."

He sat there.

"If you don't leave the Kings now, you're going to die. I can see it in your eyes."

He sat there.

"I saw the same look in Memo's brother's eyes and I told him about it. Then a couple of days later he got killed. You have to leave the Kings."

He sat there.

He didn't respond. Then they all left.

It was true, what I had told him. I had gotten a call from Memo's mom. She was hysterical. Her son had run away from home and moved into his girlfriend's house. She asked me to go over and talk to him. I did. He had joined one of the gangs and really wasn't gang material. He was a really sweet kid and kind of soft, if you know what I mean. I remember him slouching on the couch in his girlfriend's living room. Teenage rebellion, only really dangerous. I couldn't believe the girlfriend's mother would let him move in and I tried to talk to her, but it was no use. I looked at him and saw the darkness that comes into someone's eyes when they're in deep trouble and I told him he was going to get killed. He did, in a drive-by a couple of days later, sitting on the porch of someone's house.

I had seen the same thing in Ismael's eyes.

Ismael Gets Killed

A couple of weeks after I'd told Ismael he was going to get killed, he did. I don't remember the exact circumstances, only that I got a call in the middle of the night, or maybe in the afternoon, or maybe in the morning. I don't remember exactly how he was killed. I know he was shot and killed.

What I do remember is desperately trying to find his little brother Carlos. It was too late for Ismael, but I knew Carlos had to be wanting revenge for his brother. And he would get killed or kill someone getting it. I've already buried more than my share of brothers...one gets killed and then the other one gets killed looking for revenge.

I went over to their house on Avenue L. They'd finally moved off Escanaba, where for Ismael every trip home invited a Dragon to take a shot at him. Sadly, they hadn't moved far enough away. The East Side, where the letter streets are L, M, N, etc., is where people from the neighborhood go when they want to get away. What the parents don't usually understand is the fact that their kids go back to hang around with their friends. If they really want to go far enough away, they have to leave the state and start over somewhere else. Ismael's family lived in a second-floor apartment, and I went racing over there as fast as I could.

I got there and his mother and her *comadre* were there. The *comadre*, Ismael's godmother from his baptism and confirmation, was trying to console Ismael's mother. She was speechless from the grief, and nobody knew where Carlos was. I tried talking to his little sister, and she pointed me toward 87th

Street. I headed back to the parish, but had no luck finding Carlos.

I called the house a half an hour later, and found out that the police had picked Carlos up. He was driving a car with a broken taillight or something, and they had him in the lockup.

His family went and got him out, and I went back over to the house. We had a long conversation, Carlos, his family, and I. I told him he had to get out of town, leave, and not come back. I asked his mother if they had relatives anywhere out of state, or in Mexico. They didn't. I told him over and over again how Ismael was a good guy, and how he didn't want his mother to suffer another loss. I told him that revenge belongs to God.

The funeral was the usual... the funeral parlor loaded with gang members, a cop at the door, people dressed in their gang colors, a rainy day for the burial... the usual. It gets harder each time I do one of these funerals. Maybe it's because I've been in the parish a while and know the guys and their families.

Carlos left town for a while after the funeral. He's still alive.

Somewhere in the middle of it all, I started thinking, "What to do?" I'd buried a lot of kids. I'd dealt with students who couldn't read. I knew our efforts at religious education were feeble in comparison with the realities on the street, and I knew these kids didn't have a chance without a decent education. Being the son of two teachers, I took for granted that young people would know how to read before they even got to school. I couldn't imagine trying to make a life without even the basics... reading and writing and math.

Finally, I came to the conclusion that we had to reopen our parish school. I laughingly told people the decision was based on laziness. I didn't want to bury any more kids—it was too much work! The only way I could see to end the gang problem was to give these young people some kind of hope for the future with a decent education. I figured they were joining the gangs because it was the best choice they had. I wanted to offer them a better set of parameters for decision making and thought that if they had even a spark of a chance at a future they wouldn't join the gangs. It had become clear to me that for a number of reasons our public schools couldn't effectively work in this environment, and that the only hope these kids had of a decent education was in a Catholic school. So, we had to reopen the school.

When I first thought of this, I consulted with Fr. Tom Franzman, the pastor of St. Michael's. They have a parish school and I thought he'd be a good sounding board. He loves his school, but he told me "A school is nothing but a heartache." He also reminded me that it was financial suicide...something I already knew. This would be especially true of the school I hoped to open, since we didn't want to turn anyone away simply because they couldn't pay tuition. I also knew we would be transforming a parish that ran "in the black" into a place that couldn't make ends meet. Still, what else could we do?

I talked to the finance committee and they agreed. Reluctantly. After all, we were on easy street financially. We had managed to double our Sunday collections, we had some rental monies coming in from different buildings, and we had some cash in the bank. What reasonable person would open a vein and take on the financial hemorrhage of a school? But there didn't seem to be any alternative, and it seemed to be what the Lord wanted done.

The only way this could be even remotely possible would be to find a group of nuns to come and teach for slave wages. I knew this wouldn't go over too well with some parts of the church here in Chicago, but...oh well. The only way the Irish and Polish and German and other immigrant groups had ever made it was through the sacrifices of nuns. All the other immigrant groups arriving in Chicago had gotten two or three generations of "free" education through the church in the late 1800s. Why not these Mexicans?

And so I found some nuns to come and teach. By God's grace I'd hired as part-time director for our religious education program a woman who'd been a member of a religious community in Mexico. She'd heard me complaining about the kids who couldn't read and kept insisting that I write to her community in Mexico. I finally did, and the sisters there agreed to come and visit. It turned out that they were looking for a mission somewhere, and we were in competition with places like Bolivia and perhaps sub-Saharan Africa.

The sisters who came to visit decided that our kids were in worse condition than the poorest children in Mexico, and certainly worse off than kids they'd seen in Bolivia. Can you imagine? The stark reality they saw was that the kids here were dying because they didn't have a chance at a decent education, and that whole families were losing their faith.

Kids in other places they had visited might be ignorant without a school, but they probably wouldn't be killed and they probably wouldn't lose their faith. Here, it was a matter of life and death. What was at stake was the physical and spiritual salvation of these kids. The sisters decided to commit themselves to come and serve here.

Two pioneer sisters arrived in 1998 and started studying English. Then we began the process of getting students.

A New Thing for Chicago

A long time ago here in the U.S.—actually, at the Council of Baltimore in 1829—Catholics decided they needed schools to educate their children. Soon every parish was building a school, and there were lots of nuns to teach in the schools. These nuns (women religious is what we call them today) worked for next to nothing and educated generations of poor children. Since they were working almost for free, this education didn't cost the original customers of the Catholic schools very much at all. In many cases it was completely free.

Here in Chicago we have an institutional memory of that time . . . a time when nuns taught for free in parish schools. Still, for the archdiocese it was a "new" idea, since schools had not functioned that way probably since the 1940s. It took a little bit of effort to sell the idea to the archdiocese.

We also had to sell the idea to the people in the neighborhood. When the sisters agreed to come to Chicago to staff our parish school, it was the beginning of a whole process of education. The sisters had a daunting task ahead of them. One of the big problems they had to face was the difference between Catholic schools here in Chicago and Catholic schools in Mexico. In Mexico, for the great majority of people, Catholic schools are only for the rich. So here we were, telling people to sign up for a school and not to worry about paying the tuition.

The sisters worked very hard setting up little displays with pictures of their schools in Mexico. They got a photographer to take a picture of one of the little girls from the neighborhood wearing a uniform from the school. We found a graphic artist who designed some first-class flyers for us. We visited families with small children and pre-identified some possible kindergarten and first-grade students. Still, in February we didn't have any children signed up for our new school.

We decided to have a big presentation after the last Mass on one Sunday in late February. The sisters set up different tables with information in the parish hall. They prayed hard all week. We ran off flyers about the day and published it for weeks ahead of time. I had been hearing for years that Mexican immigrants didn't value education for their children, that they had no idea how important it is for the future, and that they wouldn't put their children into Catholic schools because they simply didn't care as much as the Polish or Irish immigrants before them had cared about education. This from the experts.

And so it was a big day when we opened the registration for the school. I had celebrated three Masses that Sunday and was heading back to the rectory after the last Mass before going down to the hall to see the sisters. Fr. Tony, the Nigerian resident at the parish, came running after me and said I'd better get down there right away. "I couldn't speak to them much," he said (he doesn't know more than a few words in Spanish), "but they're both down there crying."

I took a deep breath and headed over to the hall. Sure enough, the two sisters were standing in the hall, crying. Nobody had come down to see their work. Not one person. Not one child had been signed up for the school.

At this point, I was tempted to believe the "experts." It didn't seem possible that not a single person had come to sign up a child for our school. What was wrong? Was it that people didn't believe us when we told them it would be affordable? Was it that they didn't think we'd actually open the school? What was the trouble?

I wanted to join the nuns and sit there and cry. Instead, I told them not to be such ninnies, or some other idiomatic thing in Spanish, and to keep working. We set up meetings with the people from the Catholic schools office, our local bishop, and Sr. Judine, our future principal. They all told us to hang in there, and then if people didn't sign up, at least we'd tried.

So we did hang in there—and we filled the kindergarten and first grade by the end of August! We opened with these two classes in September of 1999 and have been losing money ever since. Still, the first graders can read. And they're having a great time going to school. These nuns are truly gifted teachers, it turns out. It's tough for them, since I'm insisting that they teach in English. After all, the kids have to make a life here.

One of the things I always hear coming from the kindergarteners and first graders is the sound of laughter. The sisters have adapted remarkably to life here in the ghetto. They love the children and their classrooms are happy places.

Fishers of Men

A week or so ago I had some of the rectory rats (the kids that hang around here all the time) help me clean out the garage. You'd be amazed at the stuff that piles up in a hundred-year-old building, and it was time for a little spring-cleaning. I ended up giving away a lot of "junk" that we found, including an old fishing pole.

Yesterday being Saturday, a group of kids was hanging around. One of them came to me at around noon, asking how to fix the reel on a fishing pole. I told him and thought no more about it.

After lunch, I decided to go out and work in the garage. As I opened the back door of the rectory, I was met by group of kids gathered around the porch, laughing and excited. They wanted to know if I had an eraser, the kind for erasing pencil marks.

Being a naturally suspicious adult, I asked, "What do you want it for?"

They told me they were "catching people."

"What?"

"We're catching people. We got two already." They were laughing as they said this. These are the "good kids." They'd just come out of an altar boys' meeting.

Then they showed me the setup. They'd put a dollar bill on a hook. Then, they'd unreel a hundred feet of fishing line and go hide, leaving the dollar on the sidewalk where they could see it. When the hapless victim spied the dollar bill and reached for it, they'd reel the line in a little. The victim would reach for it again, and it would be pulled slightly out of reach. They told me that a big black lady had reached for the money and when it moved she had started talking to it. "Come to mamma, money." The money jerked slightly away. "Come on, money. Come to mama."

They wanted the eraser so nobody would get hurt on the point of the fishing hook.

I gave them a little piece of wire and told them to use it instead of the fishing hook. They commented that they had to be careful in doing their fishing. "We don't want to get our ass kicked, so we have to be careful not to go after someone too big."

These are little Mexican kids fishing, and there are some big people around. They also lamented that they might lose their dollar.

I told them that when you're fishing you sometimes lose the bait.

I guess they didn't know that, since none of them have ever actually ever fished for real fish.

They spent the rest of the afternoon "fishing." At one point I heard laughter coming out of the bushes right outside my office window. I looked out and caught sight of Noe hanging out the window of their apartment on the second floor of Raul's house across the street. His little sister was downstairs, placing the dollar bill on the sidewalk. The rest of the kids were hiding in the bushes in front of the rectory under my office window and I could hear them burst out laughing when Noe reeled the dollar up and out of the reach of the victim.

Just give these kids a couple of hours on a sunny Saturday afternoon and they invent a game! The violence usually happens at night—strangely enough, in the very same spot in front of the rectory.

A Red-Light House Gets Rehabbed

After we arranged for the nuns to come and reopen the parish school, we realized that we had nowhere for them to live. What to do? There was an old convent on the parish grounds, but the place was generating around $40,000 in rental income from a drug rehabilitation group that found it an excellent location because it was big enough to house sixteen people. It didn't make sense to throw away $40,000 a year to give three nuns a place to live. The sisters had committed to sending another nun each year to staff our school, but for now we needed somewhere for three to live.

I spoke to the finance council and we decided to buy and rehab a place for the sisters. I'd had some experience with a hammer, having rehabbed a few houses on my days off, and so I wasn't too intimidated by the idea. We also had a seminarian coming for the summer. These guys have been a great help to parishes over the years...they come in, get a taste of parish life, and start swinging hammers.

I called a benefactor, and he agreed to pay for the purchase of the house. We were able to buy a brick building two houses in from the corner, across the street from Emilio's house, for $50,000. The ladies on the finance council insisted that it had to be brick so that the bullets wouldn't get the nuns. The first floor of the house was a community center that had previously been a bar and the second-floor apartment was being used by some ladies of the night. Like a lot of old Chicago houses, this one had seen lots of halfhearted rehab work over the years. Someone had hung one of those cheap suspended ceilings on the first floor, covering over the original tin ceiling.

The owners had tried to redo the apartment on the second floor, but the job they did on the plumbing was terrible and the place was a wreck. We had to open all the windows on the second floor and leave them that way just to be able to walk around, because the smell was so intensely sickening up there. Maybe it was cats. Maybe something else. Whoever was visiting the ladies at night had to be pretty desperate just to stand the smell. One of the nuns came to see the place before we started working. I don't think she believed we could make it better. It was a perfect challenge for our high-school seminarians.

Joe Boland, the college seminarian, and some of the high-school guys went to work gutting the place. That meant tearing off all the plaster, removing all the plumbing fixtures, getting rid of all the electrical wires, and taking all the garbage out. They filled two whole dumpsters.

Every day around noon they'd come over to the rectory for lunch, which was sandwiches prepared by the parish secretary and bookkeeper. The guys would be covered head to toe with dirt and you could tell they were enjoying every minute of what they were doing. They felt like men.

When they finished the demolition, they began to do the framing for new walls, bathrooms, bedrooms, and a kitchen. In the beginning, the kids couldn't even read a ruler. In the end, they could not only read the ruler, but they could work with a level and a chalk line and had learned how to knew use a circular saw and do framing for construction.

Once in a while one of the kids would say something like, "Father, we should be getting paid for this work." I'd answer, "No, you should be paying us to be allowed to work here. After all, there are schools where people pay to learn what you're learning." They would come early every morning, and when Joe had to help with a funeral or wouldn't be there for some reason, they complained bitterly. I was reminded of Freud's notion that there are two basic human needs... for meaningful work and love. These guys were getting both.

"This is just like Mr. Rogers' Neighborhood." Joe Boland said that one afternoon after I'd sent him over to Cuco's store for some jalapeños.

If you've never been to a corner store, they're something else. Cuco's place is jammed to the ceiling with all kinds of canned goods, fresh jalapeños, onions and garlic, pots and pans, telephone cards, toilet paper, dish soap, apples, *molcajetes* (a kind of mortar and pestle you use for making salsas), ice cream, Mexican music cassettes and CDs, *chile de arbol* and all kinds of other spices, and a counter where you can get fresh meat and cheese and a few vegetables that have to be kept cold. If you don't see what you need, you ask Cuco or his brother or Chemma and they usually find it somewhere in the back.

About three people can fit comfortably into Cuco's and you have to squeeze by each other to get through the narrow aisles. It's the kind of place a mother sends her five-year-old for a gallon of milk and some tortillas. There's really nothing like a corner store outside a city neighborhood, I think.

Joe wasn't used to just going to the store and getting what you need without any money. Cuco's and all the other corner stores around here use a credit system. A lot of people have "accounts," and so when we needed the chilies and I didn't have any cash, it seemed natural to me to tell Joe, "Go over to Cuco's and get us some chilies. Tell him I'll come by later and pay him." He went off without any money, got the stuff, and came back amazed. Who ever heard of such a thing?

He was also amazed by just sitting on the front steps of the rectory. This is an actual neighborhood and people go walking by all the time. It's not at all like the suburbs where people live in the back yard on their decks, if they go outside at all during the summer. Here, when your house is too hot or you just want to get some air, you sit on your front steps. That way you can catch up on all the daily gossip, cool off, and see some sights.

One of the things you see is white and black and brown people walking by, because they all live around here.

In this neighborhood, within a few blocks you can find three or four or five food stores, a few restaurants, a furniture store or two, some lawyers' offices, some variety stores, a couple of drugstores, places to get clothes and jewelry, auto parts and hardware, some goat meat (cooked into *birria* or just killed), wine for dinner, an art gallery, a few video stores, and a whole variety of other small businesses. Here you can find a street mechanic to change your brakes or battery. Here you can walk to the train and get downtown in half an hour or ride over to Calumet Park on your bike and go for a swim in the lake (Michigan, that is!).

Joe was amazed. Having grown up in suburbia, he'd never lived in a neighborhood like this. My family sometimes wonders why I love living here. They're good suburban Americans. I wonder how they can stand to get in the car and drive to everything and live so separated from the people around them. I go to visit them and we sit in the house or on the back deck. A couple of my family members are too afraid to come and visit me. I wonder how they can live surrounded by people just like them. Don't they get bored?

I've never had a problem with my vehicle here in the ghetto. People watch your stuff here. A couple of years ago, I went out to some fancy suburb for a priests' meeting. It was a three-day thing, and the first night somebody stole my spare tire off the truck. Imagine my surprise. For years I'd parked my pickup truck outside and never had a problem. One night in the suburbs and somebody's ripping me off. People around here don't have alarms on their houses. They have each other. I think it's better.

Joe was surprised by life here and he liked it a whole lot. He and the boys worked all summer and finished the demolition and the framing for the nuns' house. Things were moving along nicely. Then we got to the plumbing...

Plumbing Problems

We had finished the framing and electrical work, and the plumber was going at it. It was nearly the last thing that had to be done, and the house would soon be ready for the nuns. You may wonder what a plumbing story is doing in this book. Parish life here is very different from that in other parishes, I think. The reality of this neighborhood is that anyone with any skills (plumbers, carpenters, etc.) moves out as soon as he can afford a better place. And it's not only the tradesmen. Everyone with marketable skills generally leaves as soon as they can. As Sister Michelle from St. Michael's used to say, "The poor are poor in every way." She was referring to how difficult it is to pull together a school board, or a parish council, or anything that requires skills like reading and writing... let alone plumbing!

Then imagine trying to get tradesmen to work here. You have to see things from their perspective. They make the same money working on new construction as they do working on hundred-year-old buildings. And, in this neighborhood, there's always the possibility that their tools will be stolen, or worse, they'll be shot going to the job or on the job. So, I was more than delighted to find a plumber willing to do the work here.

The plumber had gone out for some parts and was heading for the back of the nuns' house to finish up working on the pipes when some guy standing in the alley with a gun waved him off. The plumber knew he had to get out of there, so he drove around the block and pulled into the rectory to call the cops. He was shaking a bit, probably because he was worried about his helper, whom he'd left in the basement. Bob (the plumber, that's what I'd call him, "Bob the plumber"—and he'd answer, "Father Mike the priest") wasn't sure if they'd shot his helper or what.

We went over to check and found that the helper was okay, just sort of cowering in the basement. The shooting had been aimed at somebody over on Escanaba, but still he was scared.

After the cops left, Bob started working again, even though his nerves were pretty well shot. Then he discovered he needed another part. (That's why I hate plumbing so much; you never have all the parts you need.) Even though Bob grew up around here, and even though he's over six feet tall, I could see that his hands were shaking pretty badly as he was putting the pipes together. I volunteered to get the part, since I didn't think Bob was really able to drive. I was also worried that if he got into his car he might drive away and never come back. It's hard to get plumbers, and even more difficult when people are running around waving guns.

I asked one of the nuns to drive me to the plumbing supply house. That way I wouldn't have to try and find a parking space. I thought I'd run into the place and run right back out again.

So, there I am with one of the nuns in the car and she's driving. She stops at a corner, and the guy who's been shooting is standing on that corner. I recognize him from Bob's description to the police. He's around six feet tall, is wearing a hooded black sweatshirt and jeans, and has a long braid down his back and a suspicious bulge in his waistband. The nun stops and she's talking, talking, talking. I say, "Sister, please just go." She's as sweet as she can be, and she doesn't notice the shooter staring at me in the passenger seat. She's not very street smart. We've stopped too long for a ghetto corner and the guy's look is getting harder and harder. I'm telling the nun, "Just GO!" Finally she gets the idea and we pull away.

The nuns moved into their brick house around Christmas. They were as happy as clams, and as safe could be. Thank God. They aren't always safe when they're out on the street.

A Thursday Afternoon

Late one Thursday afternoon in the fall as we're getting ready to eat dinner, one of the sisters tells me she wants to talk to me. On Thursdays, anyone who wants to eat pasta can come here for dinner. Usually there are around eight of us eating, including the seminarians and anyone else who wants to eat with us.

While the water for the pasta is boiling, the sister sits down at the kitchen table and talks to me. She tells me that the day before, on the way to their English classes, she and another sister got into the middle of a gang skirmish. On the corner of 88th and Commercial guys were shooting and diving under cars, she said, "just like on TV." The other nun in the car said to her, "Let's get out of here."

She didn't want to just run away. She wanted to call the police. I've been telling these nuns ever since they arrived in Chicago that they have to call the cops when something happens. Otherwise, I say, how will the cops even know something's going on? People in the neighborhood hardly ever call the police and I figure it's part of our job, since we probably won't get killed for calling.

So she went down Commercial and turned on 88th Street. As the car pulled up in front of the rectory she saw a guy limping along. She got out of the car and asked him if he'd been shot. He lied at first, but then he admitted that he had been shot. She talked with him a little while, but he wanted to leave. He was afraid that they'd catch up with him and finish the job, so off he limped toward Escanaba.

Chuy Ontiveros, one of the high-school seminarians, saw the nun talking to the guy. When she came into the office, he told her that she should be more careful. Chuy's afraid that the nuns don't have much in the line of street smarts.

It turns out that Chuy had been right behind the guy who got shot. This was only a few minutes before he ended up in front of the rectory. Chuy had been walking down the sidewalk on Commercial and he heard the sounds of a gang thing starting. The shots were right behind him and all he had time to do was twist his body a little bit, thinking, "Oh shit." He saw the guy maybe ten feet in front of him get hit in the leg and in the arm. Then he looked around and there was nobody there. "Thank God," he thought, and he found a convenient doorway to hide in for a minute.

He continued on his way to the rectory, where he saw the nun talking to the guy who had been shot. He tells me all this after the nun has left the kitchen and while the noodles are cooking on the stove. The pasta's almost ready. Chuy's a little shaken up, but he shrugs it off and helps set the table.

While we're eating the noodles, Arturo, a freshman at Bowen, says he saw a dead guy in the alley on his way to school Monday. I've been trying to teach these guys table manners. You know, things like, "You don't have to get up from the table to get more lemonade—you can just ask someone to pass it to you." Most of them never actually sit down at a table for dinner. Somehow I don't think "I seen a dead guy on the way to school Monday..." can be called polite dinner conversation. We'll have to work on that.

Life is different in the neighborhood. Those of us who live here know how to survive. It's the visitors who sometimes get a little shaken up.

I'll Have to Miss My Siesta Today

I'll have to miss my siesta today. But first there's the events from around 5:30 last night until now, 6:45 in the morning. It's Friday, the 6th of April.

Last night Cayita made me some *arroz con gandules*, and some turkey wings. She's a Puerto Rican lady and a good cook. Once in a while she'll make a special treat for me and whoever's around on Thursday nights. She knows the other days I go over to St. Michael's for dinner.

I went over to Cayita's to pick up the food at 5:30 last night. I was running late because I'd been caught by Don Angel, the carpenter working on the nuns' house, and because I'd been trying to catch up on the paperwork that had piled up on my desk during the day. While I'm at Cayita's she tells me she needs her windows painted, and she'll let me know if she wants me to find someone from the parish to paint them. Last year somebody from her block painted them, but he didn't scrape off the old paint and they're peeling again.

On my way back from Cayita's house I thought I heard gunfire over in the alley between Houston and Commercial. As I walked in the back door of the rectory, I shouted to a couple of girls who were in front of Raul's house across the street, "Did you hear any shooting?" They answered that they hadn't. When I came in I asked Luis, who was working the phones, "Did you hear shots?" He said that he'd heard something, but he wasn't sure what it was. So we didn't call the cops.

I ate some of the food, and I'd just finished washing the dishes when Chuy came over. He looked like he was having another "depression." He's the kid who a couple of Saturdays ago came into my office at noon and just started weeping. He's seeing a shrink for it and taking some pills to help him sleep. He used to be a member of a "party crew" that had turned into a gang…and now people were shooting at him in his neighborhood. He'd left the party crew years ago, but people didn't seem to care. That's why he's always hanging around the rectory. He isn't safe at home. It's little wonder that he feels stressed!

I took the food back out of the fridge and gave him something to eat. We talked for a little while and then I headed back to my desk to try and get some paperwork done. I managed to do a little work, and then we had a meeting of the Social Justice group. We went over how things were going and talked about the hot meals program and the clothing dispensary for the poor.

After the meeting I went back to my desk. Within a few minutes, Angel, Chuy's little brother, appeared in the doorway of my office. He and his mother had come to get Chuy and go home. "They were shooting over by Cocula's," Angel said. "There's all kinds of cops over there."

I asked him, "Did they get the guys?"

No," he answered. "The cops are chasing them all over the place right now."

He seemed a little scared, so I said, "Isn't it terrible, all that shooting." I was deliberately steering clear of any talk about feelings. I didn't want to feed his worries about his mother having to drive through all that to get back home with his brother. Talking about it would only have made him more aware of his fear, and what could he do? He still had to drive through the war zone.

So they leave, and I go back to the paperwork. Finally I decide that enough is enough and go upstairs around 8:30. I'm sitting there at 9:30 after having changed into my sweats. I flip through the channels, decide not to watch some newsmagazine show, and consider a rerun of "E.R." I'm drinking a Diet Coke.

Just when I'm thinking about turning off the TV and reading instead, the doorbell rings. I can tell it's Julio because he rings the bell three times.

I go down to let him in. He's here to pick up the window I'd had fixed for him. A kid had pitched a hunk of asphalt through it and scared the tenants in the apartment Julio's renting to them. Since Julio couldn't get the window fixed because he had to work, I'd taken it over to Economy Glass. They'd fixed it and now I had it here for him in my office.

We go upstairs and I can see that he's having a bad day. I offer him a beer and we sit down and begin watching the rerun of "E.R." His eyes start getting all red. He begins to cry a little and I ask him, "Do you want to talk about it?"

"No," he says.

After a few more times asking him if he wants to talk and hearing "No," I let it go. We'll talk later when he can speak and not break down in tears while he's doing it. He leaves and I go to bed.

At 4:45 in the morning the phone rings. I'm dead to the world, and so it takes me a couple of seconds to realize where I am. At first I think it might be Margarita, or Julio.

"Immaculate Conception." That's about all I can manage at this hour.

"Father Mike, is that you?"

"Yes."

"This is Ida Rodriguez. Phil just died." Phil is her husband, who'd had cancer and whom she had been nursing at home.

"Oh." Pause. "Do you want me to come over?"

"Yes, Father, that would be good."

"Okay, I'm on my way. I'll be there in a little while." I splash some water on my hair and find the mouthwash. I get over to Ida's in ten minutes. We say some prayers and then I sit in the kitchen talking with Ida and her sister. The house is full of people and the hospice nurse is there too. Her son arrived from the North side of Chicago. I stay until around 6:20. We spend the whole time in the kitchen with Phil on the bed in the next room. It's an unusual feeling, drinking coffee and looking through the open bedroom door and seeing Phil lying there dead. I guess we'll have the funeral on Monday. I'll have to tell Maria, the parish secretary, to wait for a call from the funeral home.

Today it's first Friday, and I should go and bring communion to the sick this morning. I have an 11:00 appointment with Manuel. I don't know what he wants to talk about. He said he wanted some "orientation." I hope he's not another post-traumatic stress guy. It's tough when they come in the office and start telling you about how their lives are coming apart, how they just start weeping in the middle of the day, how they can't seem to make a marriage work, how they want to kill themselves. We'll have to see what Manuel's problem is.

Then I have to go over to my grandmother's and take her to the doctor. She may be dying, but we'll have to see. Then I have a meeting at 4:00 with the nuns and Sr. Judine, the principal, to talk about the school and solve whatever problems have arisen. Then there's dinner at St. Michael's and Mass at 7:00. After Mass, I'll try and get to the paperwork again. The day will probably end at around 9:00 tonight and I'll have to miss my siesta this afternoon. It's going to be a long day.

"How Does All This Affect You?"

I recently read another article on post-traumatic-stress syndrome. That's what you get when you've been exposed to a traumatic event...at least that's what you can get. (There's also something called "secondary post-traumatic-stress syndrome." That's what you get when you've listened to someone's story of a stressful event.) Firemen, policemen, victims of torture and kidnapping, the people of New York City, and all kinds of people can get post-traumatic-stress syndrome. Padres can too.

The article I recently read said there's a tool the shrinks use when trying to help people deal with this syndrome. It's called systematic desensitization. I remembered this term from the psych classes I'd taken in college and graduate school ...years ago. It's frequently used in dealing with phobias. If someone's deathly afraid of cats, the strategy is to begin with pictures of cats. You have the person look at the pictures so they gradually get used to seeing cats and not having a panic attack. Then you progress to perhaps a stuffed cat, or a cat doll. This is followed by getting the person used to being in the same room with a cat, and at the end the person is feeding kitties little treats. That's systematic desensitization, and it works.

In the case of post-traumatic-stress syndrome, you'd begin by removing the person from the traumatizing environment. For example, you'd free them from the soldiers who've kidnapped them. Then you'd help them deal with the effects of kidnapping by showing them photos of men in uniform and helping them not to panic. Gradually you'd get them to the point where they didn't have a debilitating reaction to everyone in uniform and finally to the point where they could live a normal life.

So, how does that relate to working in this environment?

I think you get "systematically desensitized" after a while. The other night I was sitting up in my room, reading the Sunday paper. I had the TV on and was drinking a glass of 7-UP. I was comfortable in my chair and had a blanket over my legs. Sometime between 8:00 and 10:00 I heard a loud crash and glass splintering. I didn't bother to get up and look out the window, thinking, "If I get up every time I hear a crash around here, I'll never finish reading the paper." I'd been systematically desensitized to the sound of glass breaking.

The next morning, I found that someone had broken my car window and stolen my cell phone from the glove box of the car. I called and had the window replaced and went to buy another cell phone. If I'd stood up and looked out the window, at least I would have been able to yell at the guy. On the other hand, what good would it have done? I would have lost a night's sleep and I still would have had to replace the window and the phone.

You get desensitized. A while ago, my niece was sick. My brother and sister-in-law both called me, very worried about her. They told me how she was doing and I immediately came to the conclusion that she wasn't dying. I offered what in hindsight were some pretty weak expressions of sympathy and hung up the phone. I later found that they'd expected me to drop what I was doing and head over to the hospital to be with them. I suppose a normal person might have. I didn't, simply because she wasn't in any danger of death.

My reactions to things have changed. It's been years since I've jumped at the sound of gunfire. I suppose the normal thing to do is panic. When you live here, you don't panic. People come into the rectory, escaping from the middle of a gun battle, and we joke about it. Yesterday they were shooting outside at around 8:20 in the morning. Last night we had a meeting in the dining room of the rectory...the same room where they've shot the windows out twice. At the beginning of the meeting I jokingly reminded everyone that if we heard gunfire we should dive for the floor.

Once in a while I'll call Fr. Tom Nangle on the phone. He's the police chaplain for the Chicago Police Department. He's great to talk to, especially when you don't know what you're supposed to be feeling. You get another gang funeral and you don't feel anything at all. You start to worry... "Am I becoming cold hearted?" Then you call Nangle, and he talks to you for a while. Or you find yourself getting a little shaky. You call Nangle and he helps you get back on track.

What effect does living like this have on you? First, there's the spiritual/psychological effect. Then there's the physical effect.

I hate doctors. Actually, that's not true. I just hate going to the doctor. My old doctor, recently retired, was good.

A few years ago I was convinced I had a brain tumor. The headaches were incredible. I went to see him and he looked in my eyes and said, "Well, there's no evidence of intra-cranial bleeding... nope, no brain tumor." He told me it was the stress, and that I should get away from the stressful environment. I thanked him for his advice and went back to work.

Then, about a year later, I started getting "skipping heartbeats." The doctor told me to come downtown right away, and I met him at the hospital. He listened to my heart and couldn't hear anything. I made an appointment with him for the following Monday and, while I was getting an EKG, my heart started skipping. I said to the nurse, "Tell the doctor it's happening right now." He came in and listened to my heart skipping beats. He heard them, thank God! (You know how it is—you take your car into the shop and it's fine while the mechanic's looking at it, then you drive a half a block and it's acting up again.) The doctor looked at the tape from the machine, then called me into his office. "It's supra-ventricular fibrilation. Nothing to worry about. It's stress related." He told me to cut down on the caffeine and get out of the stressful environment. I thanked him and went back to work.

I learned that most of the "sicknesses" I get are stress related, especially if they go away when I'm not in the parish. I guess it's just common sense. About a year after the skipping heartbeats, my stomach started getting bad. I'd gone on a four-month sabbatical and my insides had been fine. Then, a couple of weeks after my return to the parish, I was getting bad again. I was afraid I'd be needing a colostomy if things didn't get any better. The doctor gave me some pills to slow things down a little bit and told me I should get out of the stressful environment. I grabbed the pills and went back to work.

And so it goes. There's a physical price to be paid if you work here. I have a priest friend who compares this job to being peeled like an onion. He says that in Buddhist thought people are seen as onions, and that life is about having layer after layer stripped away until there is nothing left because you've reached Nirvana. I'd say that in Christian thought life is about having whatever is not Christlike stripped away until people can look at you and see God's goodness. I have a long way to go . . . but I hope that whatever is not coming from God's grace is stripped away from me, or burned off, or whatever, until only the love and compassion of Jesus come through.

But, in the meantime, you get desensitized. And so there's a struggle involved here. On the one hand, you need a thick skin just to be able to survive the everyday hurts and violence. Otherwise you suffer too much and you can't function, not at all. On the other hand, you're called on to be compassionate and loving and so you don't want too thick a skin. It's a kind of balancing act, letting in enough of what's going on around you to actually feel a compassionate response and keeping enough of it out so that it doesn't stop you dead in your tracks. Sometimes things get out of balance. Then you're not compassionate or you start getting sick. It takes a lot of prayer. I know I'm not alone in this. Police and firemen and soldiers and schoolteachers and all kinds of other people have the same balancing to do. So do the nuns in our school.

Sister Mari's Encounter

I work from early morning and have a burrito for lunch. After lunch, I go upstairs for a little prayer and rest.

When I come back downstairs, Chuy, Luis, and Jazmary are in the front office. There are usually at least three or four people hanging around in the office, and only one is working. Being the heart of the neighborhood, the parish house always has groups of people stopping by. Luis says, "Somebody got shot eighteen times. Right on Commercial." Fr. Mark, who's visiting and is in the back working on the computer, calls out, "It wasn't eighteen. It was fourteen."

"You're exaggerating, Luis. It wasn't eighteen times," I say, joking around. You learn to joke around when there's nothing else you can do.

Luis smiles. "Big deal. What's the difference? Fourteen or eighteen. Still, somebody got shot."

"When?"

"This afternoon. Right now, on Commercial."

Chuy pipes in, "Yeah, Sister Mari saw it." He's telling me the latest gossip and he's excited to have the news to share.

I dial the nuns' house. Sr. Mari answers. I say, "I know somebody who's always in the middle of things!"

"Don't tell me . . . who could it be?"

"Some nun I know . . ."

"Don't tell me . . ."

"What happened, Mari?"

"Oi Padre, it was terrible. This time they really scared me."

"What happened?"

"I was taking one of the girls home. She lives across the street from those lots the parish has."

The parish has three vacant lots next to the church, where some houses burned down. A picture flashed into my head of the spot where she had been standing, and I thought again about how badly we needed to put some walls up there to stop the bullets.

"I knocked on the door, but the mother didn't have the key for the front door so she went around the side. Then they started shooting and I shouted, "Let's get inside. Run for your life!" We got into the house, but only after it was all over. They shot fourteen shots."

"Did they hit anyone?"

"Yes, a little black boy. And then they came running right by me. This time they really scared me. I have bad luck. One of these times it'll probably be me."

I tried to think of what I should tell her. She was really wound up.

"Do you have a will?"

"Father... I don't own anything. Why do I need a will?"

"So we know what to do with your body."

"Ahhh... It doesn't matter to me... you can put me in a freezer if you want!"

"Oh Mari. Don't worry. Nothing is going to happen to you."

"I feel like it is. Anyway, we all have to die someday."

The sisters aren't used to this kind of neighborhood, and the weaknesses built into it. In Mexico there is a sharp line between private and public spaces and people's homes are a lot safer. The usual Mexican house is so secure from the street that you'd need a welding torch and a sledgehammer to break in. Here in the neighborhood you can break a window and get into someone's house. Our environment simply isn't built to protect us from the bad guys.

A List of Shootings

On Monday, July 10th, at 6:00 in the evening, the ladies were in our garage handing out clothing for the poor. A group of gang members began to congregate behind the garage and another group gathered on Exchange Avenue. The women grew frightened and closed the garage doors. After a while, they got too hot in there and opened the doors. About fifteen minutes later, the rival gangs began shooting.

At 2:00 in the morning there was more shooting.

On Tuesday, July 11th, there was shooting at 7:00 in the evening, and again just after midnight.

On Wednesday, July 12th, there was shooting at 7:30 in the evening.

On Thursday, July 13th, there was shooting at 6:30 in the evening and again at midnight and at 2:30 in the morning. The shooting at midnight and 2:30 in the morning was machine-gun fire.

On Friday, July 14th, there was shooting at 6:30 in the evening, and again at 2:30 A.M. and 3:30 A.M.

On Saturday, July 15th, there was shooting in the evening and at 1:00 in the morning.

On Sunday, July 16th, there was no shooting.

How do you survive all this? Denial and repression! They're the most primitive defense mechanisms, and they work most of the time. Getting out of the neighborhood once in a while helps. Also prayer. Lots of prayer. So far, that's been my strategy.

Denial and Repression

It was 2:00 in the morning, or maybe 4:00 in the morning. The emergency line was ringing. I picked up the phone and it was Reyna's daughter telling me that her brother Juan Manuel had been killed. I was deeply saddened. I knew him, his brothers and sisters and parents. I'd thought he was clear of all the troubles, since he was old enough to have moved beyond all the gang stuff. I put on my blacks and headed for Christ Hospital, about half an hour away.

I arrived at the emergency room and didn't see the family. I looked around for them and found them in the family waiting room. The chaplain on duty was there, waiting with them for me to arrive before going in to see Juan Manuel's body. One of his brothers seemed to have been drinking.

We walked into what I call the body room (that's the only name I can think of for it). It was a small room, lit by bright fluorescent fixtures. The walls were covered by ceramic tiles and I remember seeing some chrome fixtures sticking out of the walls. There was a drain in the middle of the floor and every painted surface gleamed with shiny, off-white enamel. The room felt like a morgue. Everything was bathed in a sterile white light.

Juan Manuel's body was on a gurney pushed up against one of the walls. The gurney was about as long as the room and it left only a couple of feet near the head and maybe a foot near the feet. He was covered with a white sheet, except for his head. We crowded into the room and the hospital attendant closed the door. Juan Manuel's brother and sister went over and touched his body. They were crying. His father stood back with his mother for a couple of minutes, then I went with them and stood by his body. One of his brothers pulled back the sheet a little. His mother kissed him and picked up his head. She was talking to him. Another brother started getting a little hysterical, crying and trying to pick up his body.

Juan Manuel's mother rested her head on his cheek. Some of the blood that was coming out of his nostrils got on her face. Her husband and her daughter held her up. She looked at me with tears running down her cheeks and her son's blood smeared on her face. I embraced her and she buried her face in my chest. It was only by God's grace that we didn't all just collapse on the floor. We said some prayers together.

The hospital staff had tried to make things neat, but by now there was blood leaking out and it was getting all over the white sheets and onto the wall next to the gurney. Now I could see the reason for the ceramic tiles and the floor drain. "Those chrome things must be so they can hose the place down," I thought.

After a while, the attendants came and told us it was time to move the body. I went home and somehow slept. The next morning at Mass I was on autopilot. A big fly landed right next to the chalice on the altar. I let it sit there and after a while it flew off.

Every time I see Juan Manuel's mother, or his sister or brothers (and they're in church every Sunday), every time I hear a shot (and around here there's gunfire daily), I try not to remember the glint of the fluorescent lights off the tiles and chrome and Reyna's face smeared with tears and her son's blood.

Denial and repression. How could you live without them?

A Guy Shot in Front of the Rectory

One night I was lying in bed at about 11:00, nearly asleep. I heard some gunshots, distantly, as if in a dream. Rolling over, I thought something like, "What the hell." I was nearly asleep again when I heard the dog barking, then some voices that sounded like they were right under my window. I tried to ignore all of this, because I was really tired, but the sound of the voices continued. Usually, I can sleep right through gunfire and paramedics and all the rest. That's denial and repression for you! They let you sleep. Not this time, though.

It sounded like somebody was fighting with his girlfriend, and the dog was still barking. So I got up and looked out the window. I couldn't see anybody, but they were still somewhere nearby. I went back to bed, wishing they would go away, whoever they were. I was tired and had to go for a "family picture" in the morning. Somebody, maybe my sister or brother, had gotten the idea that we should have a portrait done. I was lying in bed, more or less awake and being kept that way by the voices.

Then I head sirens coming from far away. Rolling over, I opened my eyes and glanced at the window. I could see flashes of red light. Suddenly the sound of the sirens, which had grown louder and louder, abruptly stopped. I got up and looked out the window. A fire truck, a police car, and an ambulance had stopped right in front of the rectory. I couldn't see the heart of the action because of the angles, but I figured it had to be somewhere in front of my house. Then the paramedics came walking out from the entrance of the rectory with a young guy.

I was staring extra hard to see if I knew him. I didn't. He looked like a skinny white guy. I heard one of the paramedics say to one of the cops, "Shot twice in the legs. He'll be all right." I stood there watching for a while, thinking, "I couldn't see them because they were right in the rectory doorway." I went back to bed and the paramedics stayed outside for a long while.

It took me some time to fall asleep. My stomach hurt as I lay there in bed.

The next morning, I go outside and find blood on the rectory steps. I back up from the building to see if any of the bullets has hit the front door or broken any windows. Everything looks okay, although there are some holes in the fascia that I'm not sure were there before. Thank God for brick rectories. I'll have to tell someone to wash the blood off the steps.

I'm reminded of the guys working on the nuns' house and how they reacted to my insisting that the windows be high off the ground. The renovation of the building involved putting a new front on it. On the advice of the finance council ladies, I decided that it had to be brick. I also decided that the bottoms of the new windows needed to be at least eight feet off the sidewalk. The guys working on the building, the electricians and the plumber, kidded me about having the windows so high. "The nuns will need a ladder to open the windows," they said.

Then one day, at about 4:00 in the afternoon, the shooting started in front of the house just south of the nuns' house. A kid who lived in the house two doors from the nuns was shot. Immediately afterward I went over to reassure the tradesmen. You have to do that around here. Someone had told me, "Father, you won't get anybody decent to come and work in that neighborhood." I had proved them wrong, but I wanted to make sure that these fine workers would not be too scared to come back and finish the job. So I went over and joked around with them. "Remember how you guys were giving me a hard time? How do you feel now? It was nice to have some bricks between you and the bullets, no?" If you don't reassure these guys, they'll walk off the job and never come back.

A couple of days before that, somebody had started shooting right on the corner of 88th and Exchange. The kids were getting out of school and the buses were all pulled up in front to take them home. There were a lot of people around, and I remember comforting a mother who was shaking and crying because she had nearly gotten shot with her daughter.

I went back in the house and Bill Brennan, our parish business manager, was on the phone, calling me from St. Michael's. He told me he had nearly been killed in the crossfire. He had been on his way from Immaculate Conception to St. Michael's when a guy in the middle of the street started shooting right toward where Bill had stopped his minivan. To get out of the way, Bill dove behind the engine block in the van. I spoke with him a couple of times after the incident, and tried to reassure him. He's very good, and he doesn't charge us a fortune to do the books. It would be sad to lose him if he were to become too frightened to come and work here.

It turns out that one of the nuns almost got killed going into their house a few days ago. They didn't tell me about it because they were thinking I'd be frightened for them, or angry, or worried. I heard about it from one of the other staff members. Then I had to have a conversation with each one of the sisters about what to do if they hear gunfire. I told them they had to get somewhere with a brick wall between them and the bullets, even if the gunfire sounded far away. The usual thing to do when you hear a sound is to go and see what it is. The ghetto thing to do is different. There are some survival skills you have to learn to stay alive here. Maria Villarreal has those skills!

The South Chicago Woman Survives

After 8:30 Mass one Sunday, Maria Villareal came up and told me something that had happened this past winter. Maria is an artist who makes puppets. She goes around to the public schools and shows kids how to make puppets and put on puppet shows. She's usually an extraordinarily joyful woman.

December had been a hard month for her. Her daughter was having troubles, her granddaughter was sick, and her husband was sick too. So, she was having a bad month overall.

She had gone into the local Kentucky Fried Chicken over on 83rd Street, and on the way out a guy volunteered to help her clear the snow off her car. They were clearing the snow when Maria looked out the corner of her eye and noticed that the passenger door was unlocked. The guy noticed her looking.

They finish clearing the snow. When Maria gets in the driver's side, the guy jerks open the passenger door and slides quickly into the seat. He's right in her face.

"I'm taking the car, and I'm gonna blow your head off!"

Maria opens her door and jumps out. She's been having a bad month, and she's just not going to take it. So she starts screaming at the guy:

"FUCK YOU. YOU BASTARD. I'M HAVING A BAD MONTH AND I'M NOT PUTTING UP WITH THIS BULL-SHIT. GET THE FUCK OUTTA MY CAR YOU FUCKING SON OF A BITCH. WHO THE FUCK DO YOU THINK YOU ARE? YOU PIECE OF SHIT. GO ON, GET THE FUCK OUTTA MY CAR. GET OUT!"

Maria told me she went on and on. The guy must have thought better of the idea of messing with this maniac, so he got out, threw her snow brush back in the car, and slammed his door closed. Maria got back in the car, locked the doors, and went home.

She told me she felt bad about using all that bad language. "You know, Father Mike. I'm not like that. I don't like all that cursing. But it's just that I was having a really bad month and I just couldn't put up with any more bullshit. I went to see Fr. Tony afterward and I told him about what happened and the whole month and all and I started crying. He gave me a real good blessing and I've been better ever since.

"The thing is, that day I forgot to pray for myself. I always pray for everyone, that the Lord keep them safe, and then at the end I ask him to protect me. Before I leave the house in the morning. You know, because of the kinds of neighborhoods I go into for work and all that. But that day I had forgotten to ask him to protect me, since I was so worried about everybody else. Like I said, it was a really bad month."

I started to laugh, thinking about how the guy obviously hadn't known what he was getting into when he picked a South Chicago woman's auto to carjack.

"Do you mean to tell me he didn't steal your car just because you had a nasty attitude about it?"

"Yeah. I guess so. Then I was telling my sister-in-law about it and she said, 'Did you call the cops?' I didn't, and I probably should have. Then, about a month later, there was this woman killed when they carjacked her car over by Jeffery."

I took a moment to digest this, and what she was telling me about herself. She was feeling bad about the woman who got killed. What to tell her?

"She should have had a bad attitude. It's too bad she wasn't from South Chicago. She'd probably be alive still."

"Yeah."

So, we said our goodbyes. Maria was smiling. She told me she was having a great day and that I should, too. The sun was shining and it was a beautiful day. Maria was okay. Beautiful days can be deceiving, though. Sometimes things happen on the nicest days.

Carlos Takes a Few Shots

It was a warm afternoon sometime around the middle of September. September days can be the best in Chicago. The weather is great, sunny and warm and not humid. The window of my office was open and I could hear people walking and talking on the sidewalk behind me. I didn't hear any of the usual shouting, so the shooting took me by surprise. I hit the floor, then stuck my head up above the windowsill. I couldn't see the shooter, but he was close. Darn close, like right outside my window. While kneeling on the floor, I called 911 and held the phone up to the window so the operator could hear the shots. She said she'd send the police. The shooting stopped, and I stood up and looked out.

I saw Carlos Padilla running down 88th Street, away from Commercial, toward the nuns' house. I knew he was a Latin King. I'd met him years before and knew he had been a friend of Ismael and Carlos. I figured he had been the one shooting. I went out on the back porch, and there was a lady coming down the driveway between the rectory and the church. She was carrying a pot full of tamales and there was a little girl with her. They were making tamales to sell for the Hijas de Maria (The Daughters of Mary), a group for girls here in the parish. The woman was a little shaken up. She had heard the shots and run in the opposite direction to hide behind the church.

Across the street in front of Raul's house, Cuco and Manuel the mechanic were standing by Cuco's green van. They'd been working on the van when the shooting started. Cuco's place is the corner store right across from the rectory, and the van is what he uses to bring in supplies for the store. I went over to talk to them.

"What happened?"

"This guy started shooting. He was right over there." They pointed to a car parked on the rectory side of the street. Manuel crouched down beside the van and held his arm up around the side of the van, making a pistol with his fingers.

"He was behind the car, and he held the gun up over the top of the car and started shooting."

"You mean to tell me he wasn't even aiming?" I asked.

"No. He was just shooting down the block at somebody on Commercial," he answered.

The police cars arrived in a few minutes and the police started looking for people who'd seen what happened. A few minutes later, I saw Carlos in the back seat of one of the patrol cars. By now quite a few people had gathered on the sidewalk. I left Cuco and Manuel and walked over to where the cops were talking.

"I see you caught him," I said as I approached the cops.

"Yeah, we got him," one of the officers answered. "But nobody saw anything."

"What?" I asked, surprised.

There were a whole bunch of people standing on the sidewalk in front of Raul's building, talking about what had happened, and some of them were making the moves Carlos had made when he was shooting. I said to the cops, "I didn't actually see the shooting. I heard the shots and saw Carlos running away. But I didn't see him shoot."

"That doesn't help a whole lot in court, Father," one of the officers noted.

I pointed across the street at Cuco and Manuel, "Do you mean to tell me they didn't see anything either?"

"Nope. They didn't see a thing, Father."

I couldn't believe it. I was getting ready to call down the wrath of God on them, preparing a whole lecture in my head about how they had to talk, how they had to say what they'd seen, how they couldn't just let this go. One of the cops sensed this and stopped me as I was walking over to talk to Cuco.

"Father, I want to tell you something. You see how we have the guy in the car. Well, we don't have a case. We couldn't find the weapon. Even if these guys all testify that they saw him shooting, he'll be out in a few hours. Then he'll come and shoot them for talking."

I stood there boiling. "So what can we do about this? Do you mean to tell me there's nothing we can do?"

The cop just shrugged his shoulders. "We'll take him into the station for a few hours."

That was all they could do.

A few days later, I saw Carlos on the sidewalk in front of the rectory. I called him into the office.

"Carlos, I saw you the other day."

"What?"

"I saw you shooting. Remember? You were right over there," I pointed to where the cars were parked on 88th Street. "You crouched down behind a car and pointed toward Commercial and fired."

"That wasn't me, Father."

"Carlos, don't bullshit me. I know it was you."

He made a gesture that told me he admitted it.

"Carlos, I want to tell you something. Be a man. Don't be shooting your pistol at somebody a block away. You might hit somebody by accident. Even if you aim, it's impossible to hit a target from a block away with a pistol." I paused for a second, thinking of what I was about to say. Could I say it? I went on.

"When you pick up your gun, be a man. Before you decide to even get the gun, you have to decide you want to kill someone. Then you have to shoot like a man. Walk up to the person, put the gun in his chest, and pull the trigger. That way you won't hit somebody who's innocent. But make the decision to kill the person before you even pick up the gun. You know, I think it would be better if you never held a gun again. But if you are going to do it, do it like a man and not a fucking coward."

Carlos left, looking a little sheepish.

Just remembering and writing down this conversation makes me shake a bit. Afterward, I went over to St. Michael's for dinner and told the guys about it. What else can you do? The logic of the ghetto dictates this response. Carlos won't listen to the Gospel. He isn't afraid of the police. There are innocent people walking around the streets here, day and night. To try to protect their lives, I gave Carlos the advice I did. Thank God I went over to St. Michael's that day!

I've been eating dinner over there three days a week ever since I arrived in South Chicago. In the "good old days" long before my time, there were five priests at Immaculate Conception. They had a full-time cook and housekeeper and probably sat down to dinner together every day. These days I'm the only priest assigned here, and so I made an arrangement early on to eat with the guys at St. Michael's. It has been a real blessing for me. Especially when the shooting hits close to home.

They Shot the Nuns' Window

They shot out the nuns' window last Thursday night. I was on the phone at 9:50 with Mike Chavez talking about his marriage troubles when I heard shooting. I put him on hold and called 911. Then we continued our conversation until 10:00. At 10:20 I turned off the TV. I'd seen the weather forecast and was getting ready for bed when the phone rang. Sr. Fide was calling to tell me they'd shot out Sr. Maria de Jesus' window. She sounded a bit tense on the phone and asked me "What should we do?" I told her I'd be right over.

It turned out that they'd all been downstairs in the living room. That's where there's a brick wall on the street side and where the windows are eight feet off the floor. The sisters do lesson planning, watch TV, and eat downstairs. It's pretty soundproof and certainly safe. There's no way a bullet could ever get any one of them if they're in the living room.

They were doing the usual when they heard a couple of guys talking loudly on the street in front of their house. Sr. Maria heard one of them say something like "It's the middle window." Then they heard the gunfire. They didn't think too much more about it and continued to watch the program on TV. At 10:00 they went up to bed and that's when Sr. Maria de Jesus saw that the window of her bedroom had been shot out.

She has a second-floor window on the street side of the house. I went up and looked at the damage. All the nuns were a little nervous, and I was too. I remembered a conversation with my father. I told him I was feeling responsible for these women and that feeling was really beginning to eat away at me. I dread

the day when one of them gets hurt and sometimes I'm tempted
to send them all back to Mexico just to avoid that day. He told
me that I was being foolish, that these were grownups and that I
shouldn't feel so completely responsible for them. Of course,
when their superiors came up for a visit I repeated that conversation. I said to the mother superior, "I know I shouldn't feel responsible for the sisters, that they're grownups, and that they
make their own choices." She looked at me as if I'd gone crazy
and responded, "Of course you're responsible for these nuns."
So much for cheap psychology!

On Friday I went over to the 4th Police District and spoke
with the commander. I managed to be civil. Sometimes I have a
difficult time talking to the police in a civil tone. I know they're
doing the best they can, but I can't help thinking the "best they
can" isn't good enough. He told me to tell the sisters that it
would "never happen again." I managed not to laugh when he
said that. I'd been on the corner of 88th and Exchange for a few
years and knew something was bound to happen again. I wish he
could actually have delivered on that promise. I knew he could-
n't, so I decided I'd try to get word directly to the Dragons. I figured they'd made a mistake in shooting the nuns' window. There
were some Latin Kings in the house right next door and I was
sure they were going for them. They just got the wrong house.

On my way home Saturday night I stopped at the Malinowskis'. They live on Escanaba, and I figured they might
know how to contact the bigwigs with the Dragons. Escanaba
is in the middle of Dragons territory. I turned the corner and
saw a squad car parked at the end of the block. I talked to the
cops and asked them if they knew who was in charge of the
Dragons. They said they didn't, since Henry, the guy across the
street who used to be the boss, had been killed. So, I went on
to the Malinowskis' to see if they knew who was in charge.
They didn't, but they suggested that I talk to Mrs. Garcia.

After drinking a Pepsi with the Malinowskis, I moved on to
Mrs. Garcia's house. She didn't know who was in charge either,

but I asked her if she could try to get word to the "bigwig" that I wanted to speak to him and tell him to stop shooting at the nuns' house.

This morning, a Sunday morning, as I was praying, I asked the Lord to help me with my stomach. I realized as I was praying what my big fear actually is. I've been feeling really cranked up about the nuns' window... and worrying that one of them might be killed. Or maybe one of the little kids coming out of the school. Or maybe somebody else. Actually, probably somebody else. I'm terrified of there being another Reyna's son, or another Memo's brother, or another Ismael.

My biggest fear is that it's inevitable that somebody else I know and care about will be killed. It's inevitable. It's only a matter of time. And I don't know how I'll handle it when it happens.

Fr. George Schopp, a friend, said he'd had to leave St. Kevin's after hearing shots and being summoned to the fire station where, a few minutes later, he anointed a couple of kids. One of the kids who died was the child of a man who'd died of kidney cancer and whom George had buried a year earlier. When the child died, George had to bail out.

George and Fr. Mike Meany are sounding boards for me. George was a pastor at a nearby parish and Mike was over at St. Clotilde's. All three of us have country places about an hour away from Chicago. We eat together on Tuesday nights and talk about what's going on in our respective parishes. George and Mike are pastors in peaceful parishes. When things get really intense, I talk to them about what to do.

I guess I wonder if I'll have to bail out when the next one is killed. I'm afraid of the pain I'll go through and I'm afraid that I won't be able to face the idea of it happening again. It's the "again" that really gets me going.

These past couple of nights I've woken up feeling like I've been wrestling—and losing. The sheets have been all thrown around and I've been feeling like I'm being beaten as I sleep.

In the end it's a question of faith, I think. Do I have absolute trust in Jesus? Partly, I'd like to answer, "yes." Still, I have to recognize that there's a "no" buried somewhere in there. Do I think that no matter what happens it'll be okay? Yes, and no.

Either I'll have to get out of here, or Jesus will have to redo my faith. I think he's trying to redo it even now, but maybe I'm too stubborn or not finished learning yet or maybe he's almost finished for now. I don't know exactly where I am in the process, and I'd like to be able to be here and not feel like I want to throw up all the time. Then again, maybe that's the way the Lord wants me to feel.

I have no doubts at all that he knows what he's doing and he knows where all this is going. I have a lot of doubts about myself. When things get really bad, I remember an incident at Mass...

Something Happened at Mass

I have hardly ever spoken about what I'm about to write here and have certainly never attempted to put it down on paper. Still, a friend tells me he thinks it may make interesting reading. I hope you won't think I'm crazy...

This happened years ago, when I was coming to the end of my time at Blessed Agnes. One of our parishioners with mental balance difficulties decided that I was the source of his troubles. He sent a few letters to the pastor saying that he wanted to destroy my priesthood and kill me. These letters were written in colored pencil... and there was some question about what to do. The archdiocese offered no help at all.

Raul started getting worse. He began stalking the sisters at the parish and he wrote more threatening letters to me. These letters were pretty incoherent, but it was easy to figure out that his intention was to eliminate me and solve his problem. The nuns had seen a gun in his car.

He began coming to Mass at 6:00 in the evening and standing in the back, glowering at me. I was sure he had his gun with him. Every day I thought I'd be like Romero, killed on the job. I'd be standing up there at the altar, shaking.

You can imagine how I was feeling. I was thinking how this was all nuts, how the archdiocese must be run by a bunch of idiots, how this guy was going to kill me outright, how all this was a bunch of crap. So, there I was in the middle of the Eucharistic Prayer, after the words of consecration, and I happened to glance into the chalice.

There was blood in there.

I was scared to death. Terrified. I made a huge effort not to run right out of the sanctuary screaming. I paused for a second, then resolved not to look in the chalice again, thinking the devil was tricking me. In an instant, all of reality started to quiver like jelly. It's impossible to describe this exactly, but it was as if everything stood still and the normal flow of things stopped.

So, I'm mouthing the words of the rest of the Eucharistic Prayer and trying not to look in the chalice. I've forgotten Raul back there with his gun. I've forgotten the archdiocese. I've forgotten everything else, and I'm asking Jesus to stop playing around with me. While I'm getting through the rest of the Mass I'm praying: "Whatever you want to do, it'll be all right, but don't be horsing around with the chalice anymore." Then I look in the chalice and, thank God, it seems to be wine again. Ever since then, every time I've said Mass, I'm a little afraid he'll start with me once more.

So far, he hasn't done that again. Once or twice, though, I've been blasted while celebrating Mass or one of the sacraments. One time I was handing out communion and I got this momentary glimpse of the beauty of the people coming up in line. My eyes started filling up with tears. There was this incredible sense of the love and compassion the Lord has for these people. I could barely keep going, "The Body of Christ ...the Body of Christ...the Body of Christ." With each person, the feeling got stronger. Thank God the last person came up for communion. Otherwise I might have ended up standing there weeping.

Once I presided at the wedding of an unusual couple. The bride was older—maybe fifty years old—and a polio victim. She was short, and twisted out of shape by her battle. The groom was mildly retarded. I think he was about fifty also. When they came in to ask about being married, I paused, wondering whether they had the capacity to marry.

They didn't have all the usual frills at their Mass—only themselves and a few friends, since their families were in

Mexico. While they were exchanging their vows, they started getting all teary-eyed. I began to get a knot in my throat and the altar servers, standing there and seeing all this, started crying. I could barely get through it. It was one of those times when you have to take a deep breath to keep going.

I've had similar moments in confession, at baptisms, visiting the sick. So far, I've been able to do the job that needed to get done. Still, sometimes I'm afraid things will grind to a halt while I stand there and weep. These moments more than make up for the bad dreams.

Bad Dreams

I had a dream this afternoon during my siesta. In it, one of the sisters was following me around, trying to pat me on the back and telling me, "It's okay, it's okay." I was crying uncontrollably, like a little baby cries. I was crying so hard that I could hardly breathe. And I was running away from her as fast as I could, saying "It's *not* okay, it's *not* okay!"

We ended up in a Jewel grocery store, or something like it, that was closed and the sister was still trying to pat me on the back and saying, "It's okay, it's okay."

It wasn't okay.

I was crying for all the kids we (the Church, the parish, myself) haven't been able to help...all the kids I've buried, all the kids who end up leaving school because they can't read and are in high school, all the kids it's "too late" for.

I can remember my dad telling me that it was "too late" for Rafa and Gabriel, a couple of high-school kids who came to me for help a few years ago. He said it would be impossible to raise their ACT scores and that trying would be a waste of time. I thought about Isaac when they threw him out of Quigley...it's now "too late." I remember Miguel crying in front of the rectory when he got the news that he hadn't passed the test to Quigley and Chuy, Luis's brother, doing the same thing. I remember the little girl who wanted to get into the second grade in our school. She's in the fourth grade at a public school. Her cousin just graduated from eighth grade there last year. The fourth-grader's mom had asked this girl to help her daughter with her homework and it turned out that the eighth-grader couldn't read. The fourth-grader's mom panicked and came to us asking us to take her daughter into the second grade. We couldn't. She was too old. It's too late for her.

It's too late. And there's an army of kids who don't have a snowball's chance in hell because nobody has provided the minimum help for them to make a life. Things like knowing how to read. And it's not okay. Kids who'll one day go to that big grocery store and never be able to buy anything on the shelves.

I know I should think about what has been possible, about what has been accomplished, about those who have a life, or at least a chance at a life, but there's this great, great sadness in me over the ones we've failed.

It's probably part of the job. If you're going to do something important and good, you have to do it for those you can help. And the rest ... oh well.

But, the "oh well" ones ... the ones it's "too late" for, the ones who'll end up dead or in jail or working as busboys for the rest of their lives ...

They come to you in your dreams.

I've found that evil often follows this kind of a pattern. How does the pattern look? As I mentioned earlier, the devil will never show up "ugly" or "scary." He's too smart. What he does instead is to find some good quality, like love, for example, and simply turn up the volume. In the case of these dreams of mine, it's that pattern for sure! I really care about these people, and the hopelessness of the situation eats away at me sometimes. In making the decision to reopen the school, we as a parish were moved to do what we could about the situation. Still, there is a whole group of kids who cannot be helped. If I pay attention to what is hopeless, it can get a hold of me and suck the life and energy right out of me. Then I won't be able to do anything at all. That's how evil stops good from happening.

It's like to a mother worrying about her son or daughter. It's natural and good that a parent worry. All evil has to do is turn up the volume a little bit and worry becomes obsession. Then the mother can't sleep, or think straight, or see clearly. She loses her sense of humor and feels her heart being torn up, and more and more she feels alone.

It's easy for evil to use love as a doorway into our hearts. And I would guess that being a mother would give any person lots of reasons to worry. Still, there are lots of parents in the parish who do it with grace. Like Jazmary's mom.

Chicken Soup

Last night, Maria Guadalupe came by to pick up her daughter Jazmary from work. Jazmary works here answering the phones and Maria stopped by at around 8:20. I was sitting on the front steps with Duke when she came by and we got to talking. It was the warm end of a summer evening, perfect for telling stories.

While we were talking, Maria's two daughters played with the dog on the grass and Luis, Jazmary's *novio*, hung around watching his girlfriend. We somehow got to talking about kids and eating.

"It's a real blessing, chicken soup," Maria said, and then she started to tell some stories.

"When I was living in Mexico, in our little town, there was a lot of poverty. Even so, my little sister gave my mom a lot of grief about food. Whatever my mother cooked, my sister wouldn't eat it! If it was *caldo de pollo* (chicken soup), she wanted tostadas. If it was tostadas, she wanted scrambled eggs." She paused to look at her daughter. Jazmary is a strikingly beautiful young woman who moves with the grace of a dancer. Maybe that's why Luis is just hanging around, standing on the sidewalk watching her.

"Anyway, my sister got married. When she went to her in-laws' house, everyone already had their piece of the chicken." Maria explained: "You know how it is, when you're poor, everyone gets a little piece of the chicken. Someone gets the leg, someone else gets the thigh, someone else gets the wing. So, when she went to her in-laws' house, everyone already had their piece. When it came time to serve my sister, who at home

118

always got the leg, they put the feet on her plate! She came home crying, and we all laughed and felt sorry for her at the same time. Just the feet! And when she complained, they put the neck on her plate too! Right then, my sister started realizing how good she'd had it at home. It took me a few years to learn.

"When my mother would make *caldo de pollo* would always give away the meat to our neighbors. W always complain that she was giving away the best were left with only water. One day our street had a baby. My mother sent ove and left us with the water again! N and she answered, 'Look at all t money at all. She needs a build you up again after with her answer, not you'll really need won't be around to on to my words. Then one of p will come back to you.' My mothe chicken to all our poor neighbors and leav

"Years later, I came here o. When Jazmary was born, my mother was still alive. she couldn't be here. She was in Mexico and couldn't get a visa. I was so sad and alone. I mean, I had my husband and all, but he's a man. I wanted my mother to be around but she couldn't come and I didn't know anyone. When I came home from the hospital, I found that the lady we were renting the apartment from had left a bowl of chicken soup on the table. I remembered my mother's words right away. I just started crying.

"The lady who left the soup came down to see how I was doing, and I was sitting at the kitchen table crying. She asked me if I something was wrong with the soup. I told her about my mother, and about the chicken soup, and the two of us just sat there crying."

We were briefly interrupted by a few shots. We heard them off in the distance and the two of us looked down Exchange Street. The kids continued to play with Duke and everyone walking down 88th Street kept on going like nothing extraordinary had happened.

"Were those shots?" Maria asked.

I answered her that they were. The two of us looked down the street again. We waited a couple of minutes and then shrugged our shoulders. Maria continued her story.

"When Lizette was born, I didn't expect anyone to be there when I was got home from the hospital. I walked in and there was a bowl of soup sitting on the kitchen table again. I just sat there and cried. My mother had died, but her bowls of soup were still coming back to me.

"Whenever I can, I give away some food to my poor neighbors. It's a blessing to be able to give it away. You never know if someday you'll need a bowl of soup."

Maria got in her minivan with her two daughters and drove away. I sat on the porch and wondered if the shooting would start up again and whether I should call the cops.

The 10th of May

One disadvantage of having a day off is having to return to a day's work piled up on your desk. As I drive back into the neighborhood from my day "in the country," I usually have to steel myself for what awaits me.

Every Wednesday morning, Jesse, the maintenance man, comes into my office five or ten minutes after my arrival and tells me about: (1) the problems that have come up around here on my day off... Father, the boiler has a leaky tube, they shot out another window in the school, the school textbooks arrived and I didn't know where to put them so they're piled up here in the hallway, the Sagrado Corazon ladies were yelling at me about somebody having taken their stuff from the kitchen, etc., and (2) the problems in the neighborhood... Father, they shot a guy over on 83rd, they killed two people over by the "Y," the drug dealers who live next door to me got arrested last night, etc.

After Jesse's report today, I answered the mail and phone messages and e-mail. I ate lunch and went to rest and read for awhile. At 2:45 I looked out the window and saw there was no cop on the corner for school dismissal. I'd have to see about that later. The commander had promised me there would always be a cop on the corner at school dismissal time. Oh well, it was not the first time the police had promised something and not delivered.

I went and got a replacement window for Sr. Maria de Jesus' bedroom window (the one that had been shot out) and when I came back, John—the "crazy guy" who helps out with feeding

121

the hungry—was at the back door of the rectory. The back door was open and, through the screen door, John could hear me talking in the office. He knew I was in. There was no way to avoid him. He started, "TELL FATHER MIKE THE KIDS ARE KICKING THE SOCCER BALL AT THE WINDOWS."

John speaks only in capital letters. He's been trying to tell me about this for a few days and we've been having a little battle over it. Every group that uses the parish hall has gotten a "nasty letter" from him when something turns up broken. He wants me to know that it's not the hungry people who are smashing the windows and breaking the switches and light fixtures.

We have a hot meals program at the parish. Anyone who needs to eat can come and get a meal. It's worked out very well, and the parishioners have been really generous in their support. I guess it's because some of them have actually experienced being hungry and they know what it's like to have nothing to eat. In any case, the group that runs the hot meals program had gotten a letter, along with all the other groups that use the hall, telling them to be careful, since someone was breaking the glass block windows in the hall. That's why John was standing on the porch shouting at me.

I go outside and see that a few of the local street kids are practicing soccer in the parking lot. Anita had started a parish soccer team for them, and now they even have uniforms! I turn the corner and one of them is climbing down from the roof over the doorway.

"Hey guys...don't be kicking the ball up on the roof."

"Okay, Father."

John goes over and, pointing to the broken glass block windows, announces, "THEY DONE THIS."

I look at the windows and wonder if a soccer ball can break a glass block. The guys look too, and they say, "It's probably bullets." I don't see any slugs in the window...but who knows?

I tell them, "If you're going to kick, aim toward the concrete here and not the church."

I count the windows in the parish hall. There are now about four broken. When the number gets up to around eight or so, I'll call Rafael the bricklayer and ask him to come and put in new ones.

I should probably tell the kids not to practice soccer here. But there's nowhere else they can go. They feel safe in the shadow of the church, and they probably are. So, we'll just have to deal with broken windows until the plaza gets built. The parish owns the three lots next to our parking lot, and we plan to build a plaza there. That way the kids can play and not worry about someone shooting them. The plaza will have eight-foot walls all around it.

I go over to St. Michael's for dinner. Fr. Tom Franzman, the pastor, starts going on about how much work the Millennium campaign is... and he looks really tired. I tell him about how I have hopes he'll be my pony, but he answers that he's probably just producing more manure. You know the joke, about the eternal optimist kid whose father decides to test him. For his birthday the father fills up the barn with horse manure. The kid sees it, thinks for a second, then jumps into the middle of it and starts throwing it around. The father is puzzled by this behavior and asks his son what he's doing. The kid answers, "With all this horseshit around, there's sure to be a pony in here!"

Franzman likes to joke around. Whenever I tell him about some worry connected with the school, he gets a wry smile and says, "I'm not going to say it." The "it" in question is how he had warned me that having a school would be nothing but heartaches.

Whenever I complain about some archdiocesan program, he tops my complaint with another more outrageous one. Whenever I get started on how I'd like to trade some of my troublesome parishioners for some of his, he just laughs. All in all, I really enjoy going over there for dinner.

I got back here at 6:30 and the stream of people just wouldn't stop. One of them was Edie, who had an appointment for 7:00. She came in and started telling me about the tough time she'd been having with her boyfriend. She lives with him, they've been together for five years, and now she's discovered that he's been cheating on her. She found out that he'd had some street women in their apartment over the weekend. She told me she wanted to dump him and I agreed that was probably a good idea. The guy's a drinker and Edie is his third "woman." As she continued to talk, it came out that her father was a drinker too, and that she'd watched her mother suffer all her life with this.

I told her I thought she should talk to a counselor, since the guy was obviously a loser five years ago and she hadn't seen it when they first got together. I suggested she not see any guys at all until she'd talked some of this out...preferably with a woman counselor. She seemed to get it, but we'll have to see. I hope things works out for her...

I do a few other things and try to catch up with paperwork. Then I go upstairs to watch TV. About half an hour later, the show I'm watching is almost over and the news is about to come on when the intercom rings. It's Sr. Cati calling from the CCD office in the basement of the hall.

"We're trapped in here," she says.

"What?"

"There were a couple of guys pounding on the doors and we were afraid they'd gotten inside. So we locked ourselves in the office and called the police."

Damn. I'm thinking that it will take the police about half an hour to arrive, and then they'll be ringing my doorbell. "Why didn't you just call me?"

She's too wound up to explain, and anyway, what good does it do to talk about it now? I tell her, "I'll be right over."

I get Duke and head out. I open the outside door of the hall and start shouting "Hello! Hello!" I don't want to scare the

guys if they're inside. They're not, so I go over to the CCD office door. All the nuns are in there, with Roselia.

There are six women all together. When I see this, I laugh
and say, "You mean to tell me that even with all of you in here
you were scared? You could probably kill these guys."

One of the nuns says, "Yeah, Padre, but if they killed us,
who would be teaching tomorrow in the school?"

"Okay. Okay. Let's go home."

As we cross the parking lot, I laugh a little and gently mock
them for being ninnies. I walk them home and come back with
the dog to the rectory.

I turn on the TV again and wait for the doorbell. Sure
enough, right after the weather forecast at 10:20 P.M., the doorbell rings. It's the cops. There are four cars and a sergeant.
One of the cops is standing on the porch and the dog is barking
like mad. I step outside and close the door behind me so we
can talk.

"Sorry to bother you, Officer. The nuns were in the hall
and a couple of guys were pounding on the door."

"Is everything okay?"

"Yeah. They got their window shot out last week and
they're a little nervous is all."

The other cops come over. We stand around talking for a
while, and then they leave.

As I get into bed I think of the comment that Paul, the as-
sociate pastor at St. Michael's, made one night. "I don't know
how you sleep at night." It's a matter of giving all this stuff to
Jesus . . . but still it takes me a while to give it to him. I'm thinking as I lie there of how the contractor who gave us the bid for
the plaza looks like he might be going belly up. Of how we may
have to re-bid the job. Of how the city takes forever to issue
building permits and of how we'll probably have to redo the
whole process if it's a different contractor. Of the kids breaking
windows in the church building and how it would be good to
have the plaza so they could practice soccer and not break

stuff. Of how the nuns are working too hard. Of how they're on edge...Sr. Mari has to take tranquilizers to sleep and Sr. Sofia is getting more and more frightened...ever since she heard the "plink" of the bullets hitting the lamppost in front of her on Commercial she's been like that. Of how Sr. Cati sleeps in the front bedroom now and how she slept through the gunfire last week. Of how they need a vacation and they don't take any time away from here. Of how they'll react when one of the little kids they teach gets killed, or maybe one of the little kids' brothers. They're getting wound up and what can I do? So I lie there and try to give all this to Jesus. Eventually he takes it all and I go to sleep, around midnight, listening to a fly buzz.

I wake up at 4:30...it's my stomach. I go back to sleep and wake up at 5:30. I'm up now and it'll be okay. Sometime today I'll have to see about the contractor...although I really don't want to know if he's going bankrupt!

A Day Later

Yesterday I went over to the contractor's office and, sure enough, he wasn't there. The secretary said he'd left and she didn't know where he'd gone. I called the archdiocese and told Bob Thomas at the facilities office that we needed to get some other bids for the job. There was no alternative. The original bid had been lower (by $100,000) than all the others, and I suspect the contractor had been doing us a big favor. Bob said he'd try and get another bid. I hope this doesn't screw up the permit process...

The nuns, it turns out, hadn't called me first when they'd locked themselves in the CCD office because they'd been afraid I'd "yell at them" for being in the building so late at night. They were right! They had been setting up for the Mother's Day thing they had last night. About two hundred people came. The little kids did some dances and skits for the crowd. They did very well, and I can't imagine how well they'll do when they get to eighth grade.

So, the nuns were working late at night... and they didn't want to call me because they were afraid I'd be angry. So they called the cops instead. Then they realized the police would come to the rectory anyway, so they called me on the parish intercom. They're like little kids, in a way.

Last night I met with Sr. Sofia to talk about the confirmation Mass and complete the form for the bishop. Before we filled in the form, I spoke with her about the need they all have to rest. She agreed, and said that the problem was congregation-wide. All these nuns work too hard. I told her I wasn't sure how they were going to react when one of the little kids gets shot, or a brother of one of the kids, or one of the parents, or whoever. She said she thought they'd probably all go crazy. I told her, "That's the problem," and explained that the way evil functions is to try and get us to stop doing good. I added that it would be terrible if they had to abandon this school because the violence and evil drove them away.

What they really need is a getaway place. Then they have to go and rest. Maybe next year we'll change CCD to a weekday after school so they can have Saturdays off. I suspect it wouldn't make any difference. They'll just find more work to do and fill in the days. The work never stops around here. Even clearing the snow.

Clearing the Snow

In a lot of parishes, there's a maintenance man who clears the snow. In city parishes, it's usually the pastor. Fr. Tom Franzman over at St. Michael's managed to get a government surplus Blazer and found a plow for the front of it somewhere.

We borrow the Blazer once in a while. It's painted camouflage green and black and brown and it's kind of ugly. Still, it works, and it's better than trying to clear all the snow with the old snow throwers we have.

One March day we got a surprise snowstorm. I spent most of Saturday plowing the snow with the Blazer and it was pretty well cleared by dusk. Still, it was lightly snowing. After confessions at 5:00 I went out for dinner with the guys from St. Michael's.

When I got back to the rectory, I decided to call our sacristan. One of my priest friends told me that in his parish they'd hired a high-school kid as a sacristan and it had worked out. I'd done the same thing and found it worked pretty well, for the most part. Sometimes I'd wonder if it wasn't too much responsibility for someone so young, all the church keys and all that, but it seemed to be working okay.

Luis is our sacristan. He's one of our high-school seminarians, and the money we pay him helps with his Quigley tuition. His job is to open the church, keep the flyers and other junk from piling up in the back, set up for weddings and baptisms, keep track of supplies, and in general do the little things that have to be done when the church is in use all weekend. One of

his occasional jobs is to shovel snow off the steps and put a little salt down so people don't slip in the winter.

Being a junior in high school, Luis tends to forget things
sometimes, so I called him on his cell phone. I guess this is the
thing now. A lot of the kids have these phones.

"Luis, don't forget to come early tomorrow morning to
shovel the snow and put some salt down. It's snowing a little."

"I'll try, Father."

"I'll try? I'll try? That's not good enough, Luis. You have to
be here early and clean the steps so the ladies coming in for
the 8:30 Mass won't fall."

I was a little aggravated by the "I'll try," and Luis could
tell.

"It's just that I have a hard time getting up on Sunday mornings. I mean to, but I somehow don't get up early enough," he
explained.

"Bullshit," I think I said, "that's not good enough. Just be
here in the morning." There was a short pause. Then I said,
"Good night," and hung up the phone.

I got up at the usual time on Sunday morning, around
5:30, and had some coffee. Among the other things I thought
about while drinking my coffee, I planned what I'd say to Luis
when he didn't show up to shovel the snow. After a while I
went over to my office and began working on my sermon. At
around 7:15 the phone rang. It was Luis.

"Where are you?" I asked him, expecting him to make
some lame excuse about how his covers had gotten a hold of
him or how the weather was too cold or something.

"I'm in the sacristy in church."

My eyebrows went up, I think. I had to quickly switch
gears.

"Oh?"

"Yeah," he went on, "I slept here on the floor so I'd be
here in the morning."

Now I felt like a heel. I could picture this skinny kid sleeping on the floor with no sheets or pillow or anything and how cold the sacristy must have been, since we don't heat the church at night.

"What?"

"Yeah, I slept here so I would be sure to be here. You know how I have a hard time getting up on Sunday mornings. I wanted to be sure I got here on time."

"Oh," I answered him, nearly speechless.

"I'm calling because I can't find the shovel."

"Oh." I was still reeling from the speed at which I'd had to change gears. "I think we have a shovel over here. Come on over and we'll look for it."

He came over and we found a shovel. Then he cleared the ice and snow off the steps and put a little salt down.

I still don't know what to make of this. It's another example of people doing surprising things . . . or saying surprising things that make you think.

Should Teddy Get a Gun?

While I was running around the North side of Chicago yesterday with Teddy (whose real name is Teodoro), we stopped into Wendy's for a burger. Teddy is Noe and Vivi's big brother. They live on the second floor of Raul's house. Teddy thought it was dangerous to eat and drive at the same time, so we parked in the lot and ate our lunches. We got to talking about whether he should get a gun. I told him I thought it was a bad idea, but he said, "What if somebody comes into my house and starts threatening my wife or kids?"

He has two sons, and he is trying to be a good father, even though he's not yet married. He's twenty-three years old, and a "success story." He was in the Dragons and managed to get out. Since then, he's gone off to school for a while and come back. Recently he started an Internet business and now he has a warehouse full of inventory. He lives above the warehouse with his "wife" and two kids. He's even started to read the business pages in the newspaper!

So now we're talking about getting a weapon. I tell him I think it's always a bad idea to have a gun.

"So what if a guy comes into your house? If you shoot him, you're going to jail."

"Yeah, but I've maybe saved my wife and kids from being hurt. You're always telling me my first duty is toward my wife and kids."

"It's pretty unlikely that somebody's going to come in while you're at home." The logic of thieves, I'm thinking, is that they're cowards.

I remember that this is the same Teddy who told me about heading out to Blockbuster one night not too long ago and hearing the "pops" of what he thought were firecrackers a block away. Then he'd heard the "peeew" of the bullets flying past him down the street and he'd hustled his wife and kids back into the house almost instantly. This is the same Teddy who was working on the little roof of his house (it's like a back porch, sort of) and saw his son climbing up on the wall at the edge. He told me it felt like someone had kicked him in his stomach. With his heart pounding in his chest he had managed to grab hold of the child. Then he took him inside the house and tried not to yell at him. The kid's only two years old and he wouldn't have understood. Teddy told me he'd never felt anything like that before and he hoped never to feel it again. He's desperately afraid something might happen to one of his sons or his wife...

Now, as we sit in the parking lot of Wendy's, he says to me, "You remember how they robbed my aunt's house? She was home."

"No," I answer him, "I don't remember."

"Sure you do. She was upstairs and my uncle came home with my dad and they caught the guys going down the stairs with all the stuff from the house. My aunt was upstairs, scared and in the corner of the kitchen."

"Oh," I answer him.

"You remember how they robbed my aunt and uncle right in front of the house?"

"No," I respond. "I just remember when they robbed Rafa on the corner."

I'm thinking of the time they put a gun in Rafa's mouth and told him they wanted his jacket. Rafa's one of our college seminarians, Teddy's cousin.

"Yeah," Teddy continues, "and that other time when these two black guys came up and grabbed my mom's chain. They had a gun."

I tell him he should let the police do their job.

"Yeah. Right. After my uncle's house was robbed another time, we saw the lawn mower and other stuff in front of a house about a block away. We told the cops the thief was in there and they should go and get him. The cops told us they couldn't because none of us had seen him. The lady next door had seen him, but she didn't want to get involved."

"Still," I tell him, "it's a bad idea to have a gun."

"Doesn't it make sense?" he asks me. "You know Cuco's store has been robbed at gunpoint twice in the past year. The last one we got on videotape, the guy's shoving a gun in Chemma's face and telling him to hand over the money. With the other hand he's shoving the door of the store closed and yelling to the people trying to get in, 'We're closed.' We got that guy on videotape . . . and the cops didn't do anything."

"Yeah," I answer him, "some cops have told me I should get a gun. They've said to me, 'Father, we don't know how you sleep in there without a gun.' I've told them I have my dog."

Teddy laughs. "Duke? He's harmless."

"Yes," I agree, "but he's big enough to scare somebody. And besides," I add, "can you imagine a priest with a gun? It just wouldn't be right."

"Yeah, Father, but you don't have a wife and kids. I have to worry about them. It's what being a father is about."

I think for a minute. He's right. I've often thought that the Church's rule about celibacy makes sense in this environment, that if I had a family I couldn't possibly work here. The first time someone threatened my wife or son or daughter, I'd probably move out. In a flash. Then I come up with an answer.

"You know, you can never protect your family from all the possible bad things that might happen to them. In the end, it's a question of faith. Do you trust the Lord to take care of your family, or not? That's why you have to go to church." I've been after him because he's been slacking off on going to Mass on Sundays.

By now we've finished our lunch and are going down Elston. There's a place that has cheap wine and I'm going to get a case. We're stopped in traffic because of the construction and we're listening to the news. Teddy is interested in whether Boeing will be coming to Chicago. A few years ago we'd have been fighting over what kind of music to listen to in the car. Now, he's interested in whatever happens in the business world . . . and it turns out that Boeing has decided on our city for their headquarters.

Watching the evening news last night, I was amazed by all the coverage Boeing got. The politicians went all out for this one and the hope is that it will pay off for the city and the state. Still, you have to wonder. You have to wonder what's wrong with a city that thinks North Michigan Avenue deserves a cop on every corner and South Escanaba doesn't. I used to think this was a police problem. But the cops are simply doing what they're told. They're decent people, overall, and they do the best they can. They're simply overwhelmed and there aren't enough of them.

When I've told the local commander I think he ought to park enough cops in the neighborhood to stop all the shooting, he's laughed and said, "I'd have to put an officer on every corner. It's just not possible." Being a little bit of a smartass, I've sometimes said in response (at "community meetings" with the police department), "There's at least one cop on every corner on North Michigan. Or when there's a Bears game, or when you're having the Taste of Chicago. Do you mean to tell me we're not as valuable as the shoppers on Michigan?"

They don't like it when I talk that way.

Of course, we're not as valuable as the North Michigan shoppers, or the Chicago Bears fans, or the Taste of Chicago visitors, or the executives from Boeing.

Should Teddy get a gun?

Another Week

Saturday night I went out to Keith's restaurant with Teddy and we talked about how he's working to set up an Internet café. Keith's is a pretty fancy place and I was able to pretend I was civilized for a couple of hours.

When I got back to the rectory I went to bed early, thinking I'd get a restful night's sleep. The night before, there'd been a lot of shooting. Tonight turned out to be not much different, and I was startled wide awake a couple of times.

The first time was around midnight. I was jolted awake and found myself curled up against the wall next to my bed, looking up at the ceiling to see if the bullets were coming into the room. It sounded like a big gun. You get so you can distinguish firecrackers from .22s, and .22s from 9mms and .38s and Uzis. This sounded like something larger... maybe a shotgun or some kind of military weapon.

The second time was at around 1:30 in the morning. It was the same thing, suddenly waking up and finding myself curled up in the sheets, crouching against the wall. Both times, I thought to myself, "You silly ass. You know the bullets can't get you when you're in bed." The only problem was that I couldn't stay in bed, since the second time I had to use the bathroom pretty urgently.

By Sunday morning I was pretty wiped out. I celebrated the 8:30 Mass and was thankful there was another padre here. I asked him if he could take the 1:00 and he said he would. In the afternoon, I took off for my country getaway with Jose and Julio and moved some furniture around. We ate dinner and headed back to Chicago. When I walked into the rectory, I found that Raul Serratos had died, so I went over to Trinity Hospital to be with his family. Raul was Reyna's husband, the father of Juan Manuel...the young man who'd been killed. I remembered the morgue scene at Christ Hospital and felt incredibly sad for Reyna. Two deaths within a year, first her son and now her husband.

I found all the nuns there, and we said some prayers with the family. On returning to the parish I sat down in the living room and put on the TV. I heard some shots, so I called the police and then went to bed.

The next morning, the neighbor lady asked me who had been killed on the corner last night. I didn't know that anyone had been killed, so I asked the nuns. They said, "Oh yes, Father. There was someone killed here last night." They had just been sitting down for something to eat after having returned from the hospital when the shooting started. They had watched the whole thing from the second-floor windows of their house —even though I've told them over and over again not to stand in the windows when there's shooting.

In the afternoon, I decided I'd go over and talk to the nuns, just to see how they were doing. They were all pretty shaken up. Sister Mari talked about watching the man die: "He was bleeding, just like when you butcher a pig. He staggered down the sidewalk and fell down in the street, right near the corner. He was splashing the water on himself from the curb. He must have felt hot. Then he stopped."

We went outside to look at the plants in front of their house. They wanted to chop all the plants down, since they said the gangbangers liked to hide in them. I was against the idea. There were tall, decorative grasses and some really nice perennials scattered among the wood chips and I couldn't see just hacking them all down to the ground. It was the kind of beautiful, no-maintenance garden you'd want in front of your house. But the sisters were insisting that the plants made good hiding places and that they were afraid to come into their house after dark.

We were out there looking at the plants when a whole group of people came to the corner where the guy had been killed last night. They put a bouquet down and stood around talking. I told the nuns that maybe we should call the police, just to be safe, but we didn't. Sometimes the gangs try to go after the mourners in situations like this one. Sure enough, after about five minutes, the shooting started. We hustled ourselves back into the house and called 911. The police arrived in a few minutes, but the whole group was gone.

We'll have to move our meetings out of the dining room again. When things are safe, we use the dining room of the rectory for meetings. There are times when we have to move the meetings out of there to somewhere more secure. Twice the windows have been shot out. Unfortunately, the dining room is in the corner of the building on the first floor. After this shooting, I told the secretary to notify all the parish groups that their meetings had to be moved out of that room.

That evening I went over to St. Michael's and had dinner. Paul wanted to know details of what had happened, so that he could write a letter. I don't think there's really anything that can be done about all this, but I went over what had happened as best I could.

Then I left for my day off, and my insides were a mess. I took one of the pills the doctor gave me to calm my guts and sat on my couch in my country place drinking ice water. The rest of the afternoon I spent splitting logs to work off some stress and make firewood.

On Wednesday I returned to the parish for a funeral at 11:00. It was for Jennie Medrano, the mother of a woman from the parish whose son I'd buried a year and a half ago. After I celebrated the funeral Mass I returned to the rectory. I knew the nuns were pretty exhausted, since there'd been shootings on Monday and Tuesday nights, so I went over to talk to them.

They told me they were concerned that people had been running in the alley next to the house, even though there's a six-foot door blocking access. I told Sister Fide to talk to Don Angel, the carpenter, about putting a wall above the gate. Then Claudia, one of the new nuns, asked me if she could sleep in the rectory. She was getting really frightened sleeping in the convent, and she'd been dragging her mattress into Fide's room to sleep at night. Her room is toward the back of the house, and I suppose she's afraid a bullet will come through the window. I strongly urged the nuns to take the weekend off, and I think they will.

Last night there was shooting at 3:30 in the morning, and I called the cops. Fr. Tony told me in the morning that three cars had come, and that the cops had talked to someone who'd seen the shooting in front of Noe's house across the street.

This morning, my guts are pretty active, but so far I'm holding together. It's been a week of nightly gunfire, punctuated in the middle of the weeklong spree by the death of a young guy on the corner.

When Sarah, our volunteer grant writer, came in to work at 9 A.M., she asked me who had been shot last night in front of the rectory. I said I wasn't aware of anyone having been shot the night before. She responded by saying, "But there's blood all over the sidewalk."

I was surprised. We went out to look and, sure enough, there were blood splatters on the sidewalk. It looks like the person was shot right in front of my window and then walked down the sidewalk toward Exchange. I guess that was the gunfire I heard at around 3:30 this morning. I hadn't done anything more than roll over and dial 911. Tony told me the cops were here minutes after the shooting, but didn't mention that anyone had been hit. The nuns are pretty wound up. So am I, but at least this afternoon I had a little siesta!

The Witness List

A couple of days ago, Sr. Mari was in the back office with Yolanda, and Yolanda was saying, "You have to tell him. You have to tell him."

"Tell him what?" I asked as I walked back there.

"They broke the window of the van," Sr. Mari said. "I didn't want you to worry. But last night they broke the window of the van."

My eyebrows went up. "Who did it?"

"We're not sure. But we think it was the same people who flattened the tires on Friday night."

"What tires?" I asked. Now I was getting worried and a little angry. "Why didn't you tell me about the tires?"

"Because we didn't want you to worry. Anyway, Claudia said it was probably from the glass in the parking lot. I thought someone might have been doing it on purpose, since two tires were flat and when I got to the tire-fixing place the third one was flat too. But Claudia said it was glass or something. I didn't think so, since there were three flat tires all at one time."

"Did anything else happen?"

Sr. Mari looked uncomfortable, and so I knew something else had happened.

"I got a phone call on Friday, too."

"What kind of a phone call?"

"Do you remember those letters I've been getting from the court? About the guy who got killed here?"

"Yes," I answered, remembering the case vividly. It was about the guy who got murdered on the corner, when the nuns stuck their heads out the window and saw him fall down and die. The day after his death we had all been standing around when his friends came to put some flowers on the ground and the opposing gang came by and started shooting. All of us ran like the three stooges back into the safety of the nuns' living room.

Sr. Mari had been put on a "witness list," and been receiving summonses to court. She'd been ignoring them and recently one had arrived saying that if she didn't go to court they would come and get her. She thought they'd come and take her away right in front of all her first-graders. So we'd been discussing what to do about the summonses, since she hadn't seen anything except the guy falling down dead.

"Well," Sr. Mari went on, "I got a phone call on Friday from a man who told me he was calling for his brother, who was in jail for the killing. He told me his brother had kids, and they had no food, since their dad was in jail. He said I should be nice. He told me a lot of other stuff, too. I asked him if he was from the police. He said 'No.' I told him I hadn't seen seen anything and I hung up the phone. I was scared. He asked for me by the same name that's on the papers from the court, "Sister Maria."

"So," I said, to be sure I'd gotten it right, "you get a phone call one day telling you to be nice to the guy in jail. Then that night three of the tires on your van are flattened. You get those fixed, then someone breaks the window of your van."

"Yes," she said, "that's right."

Those sons of bitches. That's what I thought. They didn't want her testifying, so they called her and then started destroying her van. I told Sr. Mari we had to call the police. I dialed 911 and we waited. And I steamed.

The officer arrived and began preparing reports about the phone call and the window. In the middle of writing down what had happened, he commented that the two blocks on either side of the parish were the worst two blocks in the district. I could have told him that.

I was really angry, and I was thinking about what we should do. I had Antonio and his helper go and pick up some barbed wire. They went to work fixing the holes in the fencing around the parking lot between the school and the convent. We hadn't closed the gates for the ten years I'd been in the parish, since we didn't want to deal with locking/unlocking them all the time or to give the appearance of being unfriendly. But now it was time to circle the wagons, so to speak, and so the guys went to work sealing up the parish facilities as best they could. They got some locks and chains, and by the end of the day they'd closed all the openings in the broken fencing and locked all the gates. It'll be a pain to hand out keys this week, but we have to secure the place, I suppose.

I also had a couple of conversations during the day with people from the State Attorney's office. I told one of them about the phone call and asked if they had given out Sister Maria's name and phone number. He said they had. I told him she hadn't responded to the summonses because she hadn't seen anything, and he said it didn't matter, that she had to go to court anyway. I asked to talk to his supervisor, and I told him that we didn't want to be involved anymore. I told him Sister Mari wasn't going to testify. He told me that she had to come in anyway, since the judge had ordered her appearance, and that the decision about whether she'd seen anything that would help or hurt the case would be made by the court. We ended up by making an appointment for Sr. Mari and me to go down to the office and be interviewed.

Tonight is our staff Christmas party. I think I'll pour some glasses of wine for the sisters and make them have a drink. I know I need one.

When I go home for Christmas, I'll have to be careful not to mention any of this stuff. I try not to talk about these things at family parties. You get to feel like the Grinch, with everyone smiling and kids opening presents and you there spreading gloom and doom.

The Second Time
My Legs Almost Gave Out

The first time my legs almost gave out, I was changing the bell motor. It's not the kind of a thing a priest is supposed to be doing and I should have known better, but I didn't. This was years ago. I had forgotten about this experience until just last night, the second time my legs almost gave out. But first, the first time...

The church tower has three bells in it, and I wanted to hear them ring. Bells drive evil away, and I knew we had three bells, each one named after an angel. The previous pastor, or someone, had decided that the $150-a-year maintenance agreement with the bell company was too much money and cancelled the contract. As a result, nobody had gone up to check the bells for years and the "big bell" had finally stopped ringing. Who knew how long it had been since anybody had looked at these bells?

I called the bell company and they sent someone out. He climbed up there and then came down and told me that we needed new "bell swingers." They would cost somewhere in the neighborhood of $38,000. I wanted to see for myself, since we could never afford that kind of money. There was no one to call in the parish... anyone who had the skills you'd need to fix bells had long ago moved away to better pastures somewhere else. I decided I'd climb the eighty or a hundred feet up into the tower and have a look.

The stairs leading up the inside the tower are more like ladders than a staircase, and when I went up into the tower I noticed a whole lot of effervescence on the bricks. That's a kind of white powder that tells you there's water damage and that the water's leaching the salts out of the bricks and mortar. The stairs were a hundred years old and as I climbed them I thought, "I hope the whole damn thing doesn't come down." I'm afraid of heights, and these stairs were going straight up twenty steps at a time, water damaged and a little wobbly. With each step I took I was saying to myself, "Don't be a chicken-shit. If you don't do it, who will?"

I got to where the stairs ended, and I was still below the level where the bell swingers were. As I stood on the platform below the swingers, I looked at the bells themselves. The biggest one was easily ten feet tall and had to be ten feet across. How sad, to silence such a great voice. I read the Latin inscription going around the base of the bell, and checked out the huge wheel mounted on the side of the bell. It looked okay, and the bell swung easily when I moved it by hand. The problem wasn't here. It was up higher. Oh well. I had to climb some more.

In this tower, there are huge beams in a crisscross pattern, going up to the top of the tower. Someone had nailed some boards across one of the beams, and that was the way you could climb up to the very top of the tower. So, I started climbing up the side of this beam, hugging it so I wouldn't fall off. I was starting to think this was a very bad idea, that maybe one of the little boards had rotted or something...that maybe I'd plunge to my death...and then I made the mistake of looking down. This was the very spot where the grilles on the tower were open to let the sound of the bells out. So, I looked and saw clear down to the sidewalk below. A hundred feet below.

Just then the bell struck the hour. I was terrified. I could almost feel the pee running down my leg! But I was nearly to the top, so I gritted my teeth and continued to climb. Finally I arrived at the platform where the swingers were and had a look. One of the pulleys had spun on the shaft of the motor, stripping out the keyway and ruining the shaft and the pulley.

The rest of the mechanism seemed to work okay, so I took the motor and pulley off and headed down the tower.

It took a couple of trips to a machine shop, but eventually the motor got repaired and we got the bell swinging again. It was the first time anyone had heard the sound of the big bell in a long time—and the machine shop did the work for free!

But this isn't about the bells working. It isn't about the gradual repair of all kinds of things that had been "let go." It's about the feeling in my legs when I finally got back on solid ground. I stood there, after climbing down from the tower, and felt like I couldn't walk. It hit me hard...the fear. You do what you have to do, you put your fear aside, but sometimes afterward you have a hard time walking. I think cops and firemen must experience this, too.

Last night I was doing some counseling and the shooting started. It was around 4:45. When the first shot rang out, I wasn't sure it was a gun.

"Maybe it's a firecracker," I think as I try to concentrate on what the guy's saying. He's working on some tough issues...and trying to make a marriage work. Then the next set of two or three shots convinces me to move over to the phone in my office. I crunch down a little in my desk chair, because it's near the window, and dial 911. While I'm speaking, the gunfire continues. I hold the phone up to the window so the 911 operator can hear.

"There are two people shooting at each other," I tell her. "Can you hear the difference in the guns?"

She asks me, "Can you see anything?"

I say, "Let me look out the window."

She answers, "No, get to an inside wall and don't move. I'll send the police."

I look out the window anyway, keeping my eyes just barely above the bottom of the window. I see a couple of people scrambling to hide behind a van across the street. They're innocent bystanders.

I hang up the phone. Then I go back to my chair. The guy I'm talking to goes on, and I struggle to pay attention to him. Then I switch back into the "counseling mode" and am able to focus on what he's saying.

He leaves and I head over to St. Michael's to eat dinner. I'm getting out of my car and walking across the parking lot when it hits me. Other times I've felt it in my stomach, or maybe gotten a headache. This time my legs start trembling and getting weak. I stop, take a deep breath, and say something like, "Legs, don't fail me now!"

It was like coming down from the tower years before. I had done what I had to do, but the fear was still there. In this case it was shooting during a counseling session. I had ignored the fear and done my job. But it still gets to you. I went in and ate dinner.

Back at the parish, I had a couple of appointments and then the shooting started up again. It was another battle (is that what you call it when two people are exchanging gunfire?). Once more I called the cops.

I went over to the back office where one of the nuns was working. On the way, I passed the main office and asked Ramon, the high-school kid who was working that night, "Did you hear the shooting?"

"Yeah," he answered, "I was really glad I had just gotten in the door when it started. I was standing out in front right before they started shooting."

The nun in the back had heard the shooting, too. She said, "Father, we think someone was killed."

"Why?" I asked her.

"Because we saw that...what do you call those things... with the paramedics..."

"Ambulance." I filled in the word for her. Her English is a little weak yet.

"Yeah, ambulance. We saw one of those heading toward 87th street when they were shooting at 5:00. We didn't want to tell you because we didn't want you to worry."

At 8:00, Ramon was due to go home. I asked him how he was getting home, and he told me he'd called his dad to pick him up. He lives only two blocks away, but if he'd been planning to walk I was going to give him a ride home. After he left I went to practice piano a little bit, then went up to my room. I didn't want to have a beer. I thought, "If I have one, I'll want three..." and so I sat there reading with the TV on for a while. Rafa, one of our college seminarians, called at around 9:00 and we got to talking. He got shot a few years ago and still has a bullet fragment in his hand.

"After I was shot," he told me, "every time I saw a ghetto car...you know, the junkers filled up with people...I could feel the bullets going into my back."

"Yeah, it kind of gets to you, doesn't it?"

"Yeah...it takes a while for it to go away."

He hung up the phone and I went back to my book. There was a fly sitting on the lamp table next to my chair. I didn't kill it. I had a good night's sleep.

Before Mass this morning, I went around and looked for bullet holes. The rectory didn't have any new ones, but I counted three windows in the school with holes in them. A little while more, and we'll have to call the glass company. Maybe when it gets up to six windows. My collection is growing.

My Collection

Lourdes Soto just gave me another thing for my collection. It's a tiny gym shoe, blue and white. On the white part it has a guy with a basketball up in the air and his legs spread apart. Maybe it's a Nike. I'm not sure of the logos for brand names. I leave it sitting on the table in my office, next to the blue ashtray.

In that ashtray there are a few shell casings from 9mm bullets. Asuncion or maybe Bernardine gave them to me. They were collected on the sidewalk in front of the rectory. They're brass. There's also a large bullet, maybe a .38. It's lead. That's the first one that went through the dining room windows here. It came in through the storm window, went through the inside glass on the west side of the dining room, and then through the inside window on the south wall. We have it because it got caught in the wood of the window frame. I asked Chuy Ontiveros to get another bullet out of the wall of the dining room. That's the one that went through the upper windows a different time and ended up buried in the wall. He tried, but the bullet was too far into the wall. The shoe fits in with the collection, so I keep it next to the ashtray.

A few days ago, Lourdes was in the living room of her house with her grandkids. Like lots of grandmas around here, she watches them for her children. It was the middle of the afternoon and they were all sitting in the sofa watching Sesame Street or something. Suddenly there was a little sound and pieces of plaster started falling off the wall. Immediately connecting the sound with the distant gunfire she could hear, she grabbed her two grandchildren, threw them to the floor, and lay down on top of them. The bullets were coming in through the side wall of the living room. After a couple of seconds, the plaster stopped falling and she rushed the kids into the back bedroom of the house where she stripped off their clothes. They were both crying, and she wasn't sure whether anyone had been hit.

When she got their clothes off, her grandson kept moving his foot, "kind of dancing," as she told me. She took off his shoes and noticed that on his left ankle there was a small red mark, a little line. She looked at the shoe and felt inside near the ankle. There was a bullet in the shoe.

The bullet had grazed him about an inch above the heel and crossed over to lodge in his shoe, right next to his foot.

Lourdes told me the story one night during the Novena for Our Lady of Guadalupe. In the middle of the story, she said what we all say around here when something like this happens. "Thank God nothing happened." I asked her to give me the shoe and she said, "Okay. My grandson doesn't want to wear it anymore." It's practically new, except for the bullet hole.

She said that after this her kids will make her move out of the neighborhood. That's what often happens. The kids grow up and leave. Then they want their parents to leave, too. They tell them it's too dangerous to stay. The parents answer that they've lived here all their lives and they don't want to move. Still, eventually, they move.

I don't show my collection to many people. When strangers come to visit, I don't want to scare them. People in the parish already know about these things, but they prefer to practice denial and repression.

I keep these mementos to remind me. To remind me of what people live with. To remind me of how short life can be. To remind me to get to work on the plaza so there's a place to play outside and not be killed. To remind me we're here to provide a little hope. Still, it's tough when the shooting starts before your morning coffee.

A Cup of Coffee

The police department has made the corner of 88th and Exchange a "hot zone." I'm not sure what they mean by that, but there's some kind of significance to this in the great scheme of things. What's it like to live in a "hot zone"?

Thursday's thoughts.

So, there you are making a cup of coffee at 6:00 in the morning. You've got the grounds in the filter and are pouring the water into the coffeemaker. You're smelling the coffee already and you just want a cup. The first shot doesn't make you think at all. You simply look out the window and try to figure out where it came from. You move over a little bit, because you think it might have come from over there, and you want to get some brick wall between you and the shooter.

The second shot doesn't make you think either. You look out again to get a better fix on where the shooter is. You're okay. The bullets won't get you. You don't think of the bullet holes in the siding next to the back door of the kitchen. You don't think of the times they've shot out the dining room windows.

What you really want is a cup of coffee. You don't think of all the holes in windows all over the place, in the church, in the rectory, in the school. You don't think of the people across the street who have the bad fortune to live in a frame house and the time the bullet went in one wall of the house, across the top of the bed where they were sleeping, and out the other wall. You don't remember the time they almost shot the business manager right on the corner as he was leaving, or how one of the nuns almost got clipped because she leaned backward out the door instead of getting some bricks between her and the shooter.

You just want a cup of coffee.

The third shot makes you think. You think you might call the police. Then you decide not to. You think about how long it will take them to come, if they come at all. You don't think about how many times you've called in the past and how they haven't responded. You don't recall how many times you've seen them brutalize people or the time last winter, or was it a couple of winters ago, when they left a guy dead on the sidewalk for four hours in the snow. How the cop yelled at the dog, "Get that fuckin' dog outta here." How you knelt in the snow over the dead guy and offered a prayer for him and his screaming mother on the other side of the yellow tape they'd strung up between the trees. You don't bring to mind the time you visited a guy in the hospital and his mother was standing on the side of the bed opposite you asking, "How long until he wakes up?" with you on the side where the brains were leaking out of the hole behind his ear. You don't think of the time they shot the guy right on the front steps of the rectory and how you slept through it until the lights on the ambulance woke you up. You just decide not to call.

You want a cup of coffee. You step toward the coffeemaker.

The fourth shot makes you wonder if you should have called the police after all. You remember other times when you've called and they didn't come. You don't think of the time the police had you with your hands on the trunk of a car on Commercial. You don't remember the lady upstairs shouting, "You have the priest there," and the cop responding, "I give a fuck if it's mother fuckin' Teresa." You don't remember how the Kings burned down the house of somebody who'd called the police. You don't bring to mind the face of Ismael or Memo's brother or Carlos or Reyna's son or any of the kids you've buried. It's early in the morning and you want a cup of coffee. You don't have time to think of the big question: "How could this be—we're in America, aren't we?"

The thoughts come to you at night. When you're supposed to be sleeping. When the psychic toilet is supposed to flush. When you're going to be renewed for the next day. When the crap of one day is erased and your body and spirit separate for a while. The thoughts come to you and bother you. You pray to Jesus to take them away, to let you sleep, to drive the demons out. You've tried drowning them in beer. You've tried working yourself to exhaustion. You've tried numbing your mind by watching stupid programs on TV. You pray again.

Sometimes you can sleep. Even then the dreams come. Sometimes you're almost asleep and an image comes to mind that startles you wide awake. Maybe it's something you've seen on TV. Maybe it's something that happened yesterday or ten years ago. Maybe it's just backed-up garbage. Something that should have been forgotten. Something you should not have done or something you should have done. The thoughts come to you at night.

For now it's early morning and all you want is a cup of coffee. Ahhhh ... The coffee's done. There's work to do.

Thank God Nothing Happened

Yesterday morning before the 10:00 Mass, Chuy Ontiveros was standing in the back with his girlfriend Maria. I was saying hello to the people leaving after the 8:30 Mass and he wanted to take me aside to tell me something. After I had finished greeting everyone, wishing them a good week, and all the other things you do as people are leaving church on a Sunday morning, I went over and talked to Chuy.

"I wanted to tell you about something."

"Okay." I was wondering what it might be. I had the next Mass, and I didn't want to get dragged into a long conversation. I had maybe five minutes to talk to him.

"Last night I was in front of Maria's house in the car," he started. Maria was standing there. She's a pretty girl, shy and calm. I looked over to her and Chuy kept talking.

"They shot out the windows of the car."

I looked back at Chuy, "What?"

"I was getting ready to pull out of the parking space."

"What time was it?" Your first instinct is to get ready to blame the person for being out too late at night. It turned out that wasn't the case.

"It was around 7:30. My parents wanted me home at 8:00, so I was going home."

"Were they shooting at you?" You always want to know if the person did something to bring down this kind of violence on their own head.

"No, they were shooting everywhere. They shot a bunch of other cars on the block."

I hadn't absorbed all the details yet, so I asked Maria, "Where were you?" Maybe they were making out in the car, or doing something they shouldn't have been doing.

"I was in the house." Oh well, you think, they really weren't doing anything wrong at all.

"Did you hear the shooting?"

"Yeah, they were shooting like mad."

Then I turned back to Chuy. "What happened? Exactly?"

"I was in the space in front of Maria's house. I was getting ready to pull out of the space. Then they started shooting all crazy. The bullet went through the back window, across the car, and through the windshield too. It was on the passenger side."

I looked at him. He seemed pretty calm. Then I looked at Maria and said to her, "It's a good thing you weren't in the car."

Chuy answered, "It sure is. If she had been there the bullet would have gone right into her head."

"You ought to be spending the day today thanking God that nothing happened," I patted him on the shoulder as I tried to console him. "You look okay." I looked him up and down, "How did you sleep last night?"

"I slept okay," he answered,.

I looked over at his girlfriend and asked her, "And you, how did you sleep?"

"Okay," she said, as she looked down at the ground.

"All right, then." I had to get ready for Mass. "You're both okay." I patted them both on the shoulder and turned to walk away, "Thank God nothing happened."

Since it was the Sunday after Easter, I preached at the Masses I celebrated that day on the need for adult faith. Not the kind of faith that Thomas had, the kind of faith that needs proof to believe, but the faith of those who have not seen and have believed.

After my last Mass for the day, I saw Chuy's mother. I asked her if she knew what had happened and she told me she did. "What can you do?" was about all she said, followed by something like, "Thank God nothing happened."

The neighborhood is the kind of place where someone shooting out the windows of your car with you in it falls into the category of "nothing happened." As I was praying this morning about all this, and what to do, it occurred to me that there isn't much I *can* do.

It enrages you, and saddens you, and sucks the life out of you. At the very least, though, I thought, you can be a witness and tell the story.

I Don't Usually Kill Flies

When I was a new padre, I was nearly killed in a shoot-out near St. Mark's parish. Thank God I had a retreat scheduled right after that incident. You might remember that from the beginning of the book. I wanted to tell you about that retreat. I hope you don't think I'm crazy.

I've been going on a silent retreat every year for the past twenty-two years... and once I even did the thirty-day silent retreat St. Ignatius calls for! And then there was the one in the West Bank in Israel... the nightly gunfire made me feel right at home, but that's another story.

This early retreat was a difficult one. I was a new priest and things weren't going well for me. Part of the reason for the silence in these retreats, I think, is so that the noise of ordinary day-to-day living can gradually die out and you can listen to what's in your heart more carefully.

I had spent a couple of days sleeping and eating... and praying a little. I was resting up and kind of purging my spirit of all the garbage that had accumulated. Part of the Spiritual Exercises involves praying before a crucifix. I generally try to avoid that kind of prayer. For me, prayer is a "Technicolor" experience. I can imagine Jesus on the cross, still alive, and dying. I can imagine the smells of feces from other people who've died on the same cross. I can imagine the dried blood. I can imagine the people walking by, indifferent to what is happening. I can imagine the sounds of the place. I can imagine the flies buzzing around. All this, and more. It's a problem when you have a good imagination and you're trying to imagine something terrible.

So, there I was, imagining this, and I couldn't keep praying. I didn't want to look at death and I felt an instinctive dread of what I was supposed to be praying about. I was avoiding something. And so I told Jesus I was afraid. And the more I prayed about it, the more it became clear to me just how afraid I was. And we were talking there, I was praying, and he asked me what I was afraid of.

I told him I'd almost been killed and I was secretly terrified. I vividly remembered the tricycle wheel spinning right next to my head as I lay on the sidewalk and the shots that passed right over the top of me. I felt again the utter and complete desolation on the street. There was nobody, nobody around at all. I told him that the worst thing I could imagine was to bleed to death on the sidewalk and have no one there. I didn't want to die alone, shot by someone and conscious of everything around me and conscious that I was bleeding to death and completely abandoned. I told him I didn't think I could go back to work at St. Mark's, or anywhere else where I might be randomly killed. I was filled with terror.

There. It was out. At least I could name the biggest fear I had, and I tried to go back to praying. Still, I was scared. But at least I could talk to him about it. While I was praying, he told me not to worry, that he'd be there.

I wasn't convinced. It was really eating at me, this fear.

He told me to remember that the last sense you lose as you're dying is your sense of hearing. I remembered that from having worked as a hospital chaplain while I was in the seminary. In our training for this work we were told to be careful of what we said around people in comas, because they sometimes wake up and remember what others were saying around them.

He reminded me that the last sense I'd lose, after my senses of sight and taste and smell and touch were gone, as I lay bleeding to death on the street somewhere, unable to move, would be my sense of hearing.

I said something like, "So what?" I often have a smart mouth on me when I'm praying.

Then he promised me that the very last thing I would hear as I died, no matter what, would be a tiny sound.

It would be a fly buzzing. It would be him.

I wouldn't be alone.

Not to worry.

I'm not alone.

A Wound in the Body of Christ

It takes a while for a book to be born. I began writing this book four years ago, before the priest pedophilia disaster hit the news...perhaps in an age of innocence. Or perhaps it wasn't so innocent after all.

I arrived in South Chicago in 1993 and remember the first time I heard confessions here. Sometime in the 1970s they had taken out the confessionals and replaced them with "reconciliation rooms." I sat in a reconciliation room once and decided I'd never do it again. There was no window in the room, and all someone had to do would be to enter the room, stand there a couple of minutes, then run out screaming that I'd grabbed their petuta. After that one time, I always heard confessions in the church with a little kneeler that had a screen for privacy. It's not that I'm paranoid—but I love being a priest and want to avoid any possible situation that might put me at risk.

It's with some sadness that I reread this manuscript. A lot of what I used to enjoy doing was working with the kids. I guess over the past few years I've distanced myself from that work, little by little. They no longer hang around the house here. Nobody comes here to do homework. We have reopened the school, and I hardly ever go over there. I don't work at all with the altar servers. At one time in the distant past I used to go on overnight retreats with the different youth groups... always with chaperones, and never alone with any kid (I guess I've always been a little nervous about that stuff). These days I wouldn't think of going on an overnight with any kids. We used to have two youth groups in the parish, a "Jovenes" group that spoke Spanish, and an English-speaking group. Of the two, the English speakers were the more troubled population . . . not Mexican, and not American, they were a population very much at risk for gang involvement. They required constant attention and supervision. I used to have to drive some of them home from the meetings so they wouldn't get shot walking home.

We don't have an English-speaking group any more, and I have not attended a Jovenes meeting in a couple of years. We no longer have Thursday spaghetti nights here. I could go on and on.

It's a real sadness and loss for me, and I think for the parish. Some of my identity was as a "father" to these young people, who may have had a missing father or one who had an addiction problem or other troubles. Some of these kids simply needed a healthy male figure around, someone who isn't their dad and who can give them a different perspective on their struggles.

I am saddened for the victims of the pedophiles . . . and I include myself, other padres, the bishops, and the whole Body of Christ. I think every sin has a social dimension and we all pay the price when any one of us falls. I think there's something in St. Paul about that. Someday I hope innocence will be restored to the Church. But I think probably not in my lifetime.

Final Thoughts
What Any Reasonable Person Would Do

I had a conversation recently with my spiritual director. I've had the same spiritual director for twenty-two years now, and he knows me pretty well. Once, he told me I had a "unique perspective." I guess it's true, but human nature being what it is, I sometimes think that everyone thinks the way I do. Then I wonder.

I usually believe that any reasonable person, given the realities of life, would come to the same conclusions I've come to, and be doing something similar to what I'm doing. That should tell you how crazy I am! Still, I'd like to share with you the way I see life after eighteen years being a priest in tough situations.

I think "freedom"—at least the way we usually think of it—is an illusion. As far as I can tell, absolute freedom doesn't exist. I think we all have some measure of freedom, but in the end we have to choose who or what will be our master. For some people it's their Lexus or their big house or their love of gourmet food or their music. For some people it's their career. For some people it's their family. It's a question of what you want to give your life to, or for.

I can remember a conversation with one of my close friends during my seminary days. He told me he had come to the conclusion that it didn't matter to the Lord what he did with his life. He could be a priest, or not, and it wouldn't matter to God. I was shocked. I had come to exactly the opposite conclusion. He's one of the guys who left the priesthood, by the way...

How do you come to the conclusion that you want to spend your life doing what I do? I think there is one necessary step you have to take, and one underlying "presupposition" you have to have.

That step, I think, involves beginning by sorting out what really matters from what is not so important. I think the pace of our lives makes us numb and we (and I include myself in this) cannot distinguish what's important and worth the worry from what's secondary in the big scheme of things. I find it a constant struggle to hang on to the big questions and ignore things like the traffic when I'm driving, or worrying about money, or the details of everyday living, or the gunfire that's a part of life where I live.

Part of the process of this "sorting out" has to do with distancing yourself from the immediate distractions and trying to focus. The only way I've been able to do this is to spend some time alone in silence. I feel sorry for people who have no way to get distance and silence in their lives.

Once you begin to straighten out your priorities, then you have to look at your thinking. You have to decide whether there's a "plan" or not. In other words, is life random and meaningless, or is there an order to things? I don't know how anyone can look around at the tremendous order in nature and believe that there's not some kind of intelligence behind what they see. I sometimes think people avoid thinking about this because of the implications for their personal lives and decisions. What do I mean?

If you look around and see order, then you have to conclude, reasonably I think, that someone or something has created this order. Then the next step, logically, is to recognize that you are a part of this order. Then you have to begin to ask yourself what your part in all this should be, I think.

And that's where things start getting difficult. If there's order out there in creation and you're a part of creation, you have a place where you fit in. In other words, there's something you should be doing! And it matters what you do.

I think we all grasp this on the level of the environment. We all know that we can't dump poisons into our drinking water, that what we do collectively makes a difference in the quality of our lives. We have a harder time with the individual decisions we make. I suppose many people think, "How can my personal decision make a difference?" It's a perspective I really don't understand very well. If you are a part of an ordered universe, how could your personal decision *not* make a difference? And so it goes. If you believe that God exists and has a plan for creation, you have a part in that plan. It's really not all that complicated, I think. That's the "presupposition," that there is order out there and that you are a part of that order.

I believe that the Lord has a definite plan for what he wants each person to do. That's God's order for things. In one sense, the Kingdom of God is here. In another sense, it's been growing for a couple of thousand years, and it's coming closer. Sometimes, in my better moments, I see the violence in the neighborhood as the birth pains of the Kingdom. And I see that remarkable things are happening!

Eighteen years ago, I lay on the floor at my ordination and I was terrified. It hasn't been easy, being a priest. It hasn't been easy, hanging on to my place in the order of the universe. Still, I think I'm coming close to the way the Lord wants me to live. At least occasionally. Every once in a while, by God's grace, I get the sense that I'm doing exactly the right thing at exactly the right time. What a joy! What peace! To find what you're supposed to be doing and do it.

I hope you find the same thing.

A Note of Thanks

A few thank you's are in order. Thanks to Father Andy Greeley, who was kind enough to read the beginnings of my first book and encouraged me to write *Daisies in the Junkyard*. To Bob and Susan Gleason, who worked with me on the manuscript and encouraged me to continue writing. To Father Mark Bartosic for his kind reading of this book in a very rough form. To all the padres and other people who have helped and supported me along the way. To Robert Ellsberg and Catherine Costello at Orbis Books, who have been a real joy to work with. And to Celine Allen for the care she took in copyediting the manuscript. Where would we be without the kindness of other people?